For more information about membership in
The Order of Sustainable Faith visit *theorderSF.org*

Invitations & Commitments
A RULE OF LIFE

The Order Of
Sustainable Faith

a missional monastic expression
for the Vineyard Movement

jared patrick boyd

A LETTER FROM PHIL STROUT

I remember the first time I met Jared Boyd, when he shared his vision for a monastic expression related to the Vineyard. I listened as he explained his heart for a healthy rhythm of life. He mentioned the need to help our church planters learn a healthy lifestyle before planting. I liked the idea from the beginning. To hear an outside-of-the-box vision articulated with clarity of formation and mission, work and solitude, life and laughter, giving and receiving—sounded so right, and I felt he was onto something.

That was a couple of years ago. Now, as the time of implementation draws near, I for one am really cheering for the Boyd family and the entire group that has felt called to undertake this monastic assignment. I would not use the word adventure; I choose to say *assignment*, as it specifies something particular— with an outcome in mind. God has given some fresh vision and ideas, and I believe God will help these folks walk it out.

Phil Strout
National Director
Vineyard USA

AN INTRODUCTION

During Holy Week of 2012 a group of Vineyard pastors and national leaders gathered at a hospitality house in Norwood, Ohio known as The Convent. This former living quarters for the Sisters of Charity has, since 2007, been a place of rest and retreat for pastors and lay-leaders in the Vineyard. Dave and Jody Nixon, through their ministry Sustainable Faith, have operated The Convent as a place of hospitality for those who lead— leaders who are often worn thin and in need of care as part of a rhythm of ministry to others.

The Holy Week gathering came at the invitation of my wife Jaime and me. The two questions that we brought forth during a three-day discernment retreat were these: 1) Is there room in The Vineyard for a *monastic expression*? 2) If there *is* room, what might such an expression look like?

In the year prior to this gathering, we had begun to think about church-planting in the Pacific Northwest when a series of prophetic words and dreams confirmed that the vision that God was stirring in me was a vision to plant a Vineyard Monastery. As this vision began to take root, I shared it with my wife, a few close friends, and my spiritual director. Mostly, I prayed and waited for God to reveal more.

The Vineyard has historically been a *renewal* movement. John Wimber encouraged us to "take the best and go." He was, of course, encouraging us to take what he and others had birthed through the

Vineyard Movement, and to build upon it. Vineyard pastors all over the world are trying to do just that. With a deep love for Jesus and a commitment to the theology and practice of the Kingdom of God, pastors and leaders are creatively working out what it means in their present context to do what Jesus did.

Over the past number of years, what has begun to emerge throughout the Vineyard is our great need to be more closely attentive to the movements in our life: body, soul, and spirit. We have more frequently, and with greater intentionality, borrowed from models of church and spiritual formation that take us back to ancient practices in the care of souls. Hundreds of Vineyard members are praying the Divine Hours, scores of pastors and leaders are making their way through the Spiritual Exercises of St. Ignatius, dozens are being trained in the ancient charism of Spiritual Direction. We are learning that there is always an invitation from God to more deeply realize his love and his great affection for us. We are learning that it is from this deep place that great leadership is birthed. It is from the humility that accompanies it that longevity in leadership is governed.

It is no great coincidence that before St. Ignatius of Loyola did the things that we remember him for —prior to going to Rome or empowering others to teach and lead—he convalesced in a bed for nearly a year and wept and prayed long hours over the life of Christ and the *Lives of the Saints*. If an institution such as the Vineyard can learn together, and I believe that we can, what we are learning is more of what

Wimber taught us early on— it is the *experience of God* that empowers us for the work of the Kingdom. It is the *experience of God* that sustains faith over the long haul. Wimber taught us how to worship, and out of that worship flowed healing and prophecy. It is also no great coincidence that before John Wimber lead with prophetic power and healing ministry, he learned to sit quietly in a Quaker meeting. It is my opinion that a deeper *experience of God* is being nurtured in the Vineyard through the contemplative life. Perhaps we can take John Wimber's admonition to "take the best and go!" and extend it beyond the Vineyard, reaching back for the best of the *contemplative life*— chewing the meat and spitting out the bones.

It is in this spirit of *taking the best* of the historic church and from within the stream of a *renewal movement* that I write this brief introduction and invitation to membership in The Order of Sustainable Faith, a missional monastic expression for the Vineyard. Monastic communities have always served the church to both help deepen the experience of God in the world, and to empower great risk for the growth of the Church— both of which have as their end nurturing lives that follow after Jesus. Monasticism has given us models of work and prayer, silence and solitude, mission and hospitality. Religious orders have demonstrated for us a model of solidarity among members who are spread all over the world engaged in the work of bringing good news to the poor and creating contexts where captives can be set free.

The Order of Sustainable Faith invites those who wish to engage more deeply in the contemplative life, in service and submission to the *Missio Dei*. It is our hope to prepare leaders, pastors, and lay-people to discern what God has uniquely invited them to do, to nurture the courage and faith to do it, and to surface a humility that will allow them to do it their entire life. In the pursuit of expanding Christ's Church into the world, may we learn the discipline of not growing weary in doing good.

Throughout history, monasticism has taken two forms: 1) *Cloistered orders*, such as the Benedictines and Cistercians (among others), and 2) non-cloistered *preaching orders* (sometimes referred to as Mendicant orders)— the Franscicans, Dominicans, Augustinians, and Jesuits.[1] Cloistered orders live together in a semi-hermetical living quarters. They share life together while also pursuing a life of silence and solitude, a life that is deeply tied to the land. This is what most people think of when they think of a monastery. They think of Thomas Merton at the Abbey of Gethsemane whose written work and life served to deepen the faith of so many in the second half of the last century. Members in a cloistered order value the stability that is found in the cloistered community, and they commit to living under a *rule of life*, the most popular of which has been The Rule of St. Benedict.

---

[1] These four orders began in a non-cloistered form with men, in particular, traveling as preachers while begging for their provisions. Eventually, many of these orders also moved to a more cloistered form.

Members of Mendicant orders are sometimes cloistered, though often are not. Members in these historically more *missional* orders are often spread throughout the world, doing work together such as teaching in a school (Jesuits) or opening up a medical clinic (Franciscans). The founders of these orders in particular, Ignatius of Loyola and St. Francis of Assisi, both began missional monastic movements that addressed the needs of the poor and poor in Spirit, alike. Members of the mendicant orders are committed to a way of life, and often a rule of life, though, rather than committing to live in one place, their placement in the world is lead by the Holy Spirit and a leadership structure that gives members "assignments" in the world.

We believe that it is within the ethos of the Vineyard to glean the best of both of these structures. We will simply call these the *Residential Expression* and the *Non-Residential Expression* respectively. Additionally, there is a hybrid membership that we are calling the *Domestic Expression*. There is more inside these pages that will help to orient you to our thinking on these expressions.

There are three things at the heart of The Order of Sustainable Faith, and these are connected to the vision for discovery of each individual member's vocation and/or *charism* in the Kingdom of God:[2]

  1. The work of the Holy Spirit,
  2. a commitment to Spiritual Direction,
  3. in the context of a discerning community.

---

2   For an overview of how we use the word vocation and the word charism in this work, please see section 6.1 On Vocation & Charism.

You will find in this *Rule of Life* a brief outline of how each type of membership is articulated. Additionally, you will find a list of *commitments*. These commitments are simply areas of life (discipleship) to which we are committed to examining in the context of meeting with a spiritual director. You will notice that there is nothing new here. This is simply an *invitation* to more deeply commit to many of things we in The Vineyard are leaning into already. It is expected that each member's expression and articulation of this rule of life will differ. God's command comes to each of us in our own unique particularity.[3]

We begin by inviting you into our *Non-Residential Expression*. At the time I write this, we are actively looking and praying for land and resources in order to build a Residential Community that is committed to the stability of a specific place, and with a deep connection to the work of the land and to the work of *sustainable agriculture*.[4] Additionally, we are beginning conversations in multiple regions (in both urban and rural locations) where we hope one-day future Vineyard monasteries might be planted.

At the conclusion of our 2012 Holy Week gathering we made clear our commitment to the Vineyard and our desire to launch a missional monastic expression under the authority structure of Vineyard Church Planting. One of the criticisms

---

3   Karl Barth. *Church Dogmatics*. II/2 § 38

4   It is intended that the work of sustainable agriculture will emerge as a prominent charism of The Order of Sustainable Faith. Our decision to place the first Residential Community on a piece of land—where we will work toward a permaculture model of food production—is intentional.

of the "new monastic" movement is that it can often lack a rootedness in a larger structure or institution. We love the Church in all shapes and expressions. Our leaning toward *missional community* and monasticism is not because we think it makes for a better way of doing it— we just feel deeply invited by God to pursue this. Our greatest desire is to serve the church and the work of people following Jesus and his kingdom.

Our journey in birthing a monastic expression within the Vineyard has been intentionally slow and informed by voices and conversations that are too numerous to include even in passing. We are indebted to the wisdom of so many who have spoken life into this vision, whose prophetic words have nurtured the process of discernment, and whose prayers will continue to hold us up. Some of those people have offered their words of encouragement for the Monastic Expression as well as their thoughts on the Vineyard, the contemplative and active life, and spiritual direction. A number of these follow this letter.

We pray that we have stewarded this vision well up to this point. It is our hope that through this journey the Spirit will give life, and your charism will emerge.

Blessings to you,

jared patrick boyd
On Behalf of The Boyd Family
The Eve of Advent 2013
St. Francis Retreat Center
Mepkin Abbey

During my many retreats to the Abbey of Gethsemani almost 20 years ago, the hope and longing for a new monastic order took root in me. I journaled about and prayed for the emergence of a modern day monastic order: one that combined communal rhythms of meaningful work and regular prayer, an appreciation for the intellectual life, a practice of the charismatic dimension of faith, and a missional stance — all anchored in a wise and practical Rule of Life. I believe those prayers, longings, and hopes are being specifically answered in The Order of Sustainable Faith, and I believe my friend and brother Jared Boyd has been called to lead this new expression.

-Dave Nixon, Director, Sustainable Faith

The justice of the Kingdom has been a key element in most monastic expressions through the history of the Church. Whether it be the foundational connection with the land in all of the initial monastic orders, or the pursuit of social and economic justice in mendicant orders like the Franciscans, the kind of justice the Lord tells us to seek is a holistic calling. As I have journeyed with Jared and his family, discerning the calling the Lord has given them, the realization of how significant this work they have been called into is breathtaking. Not only do I genuinely resonate with the vision for a monastic expression within the Vineyard movement, but I see its future being deeply influential for sowing justice in the Vineyard both now and in generations to come.

— Steven Hamilton, Steering Committee, Vineyard Justice Network

I came to the Order of Sustainable Faith as an outsider to the contemplative and monastic tradition. Through Jared Boyd's leadership, I was introduced to a variety of practices and resources that grew the foundation of my inner self. Previously, most of my focus on faith and leadership was derived from external strategies that were beginning to dwindle in their effectiveness. I was burned out in my personal faith and motivation to pastor. The spiritual direction, group discussion and listening, retreats, and contemplative practices that are a part of The Order have served to get me in touch with God and myself. I have seen the reality that the best way for me to care for my congregation is to first care for my relationship with God and myself. This includes pursuing understanding of my identity, gifting, and vocation as well as understanding my brokenness and false selves. Participation in the Order is a commitment well worth the time and energy. The fruit of the practices are evident in every area of my life and ministry.

-- *Paige Bailey, Pastor*

One of our great desires in the Vineyard is to multiply disciples, leaders and churches. We want to train and release men and women who deeply and personally embody the heart of Jesus and his kingdom, who will not only live transformed lives themselves, but will bring the transformational presence of Christ to every area of society, and who will engage in fruitful ministry and leadership throughout their entire lives. This kind of life requires a very strong foundation, a sustainable faith. I love the way Jared Boyd is envisioning and working to accomplish this through a monastic expression in the larger Vineyard movement. Bring it on! And may we bring the presence and power of Christ's kingdom to every part of our world.

-- *Michael Gatlin, National Coordinator,*
  Multiply Vineyard

Modern American Christians have often bought into a false division between contemplation vs. action, learning vs. doing, "theory" vs. "practice." Orthodox Christianity has always claimed that people are designed by God to live both/and lives of contemplation and action — learning and doing — so that they can best aim at the abundant, flourishing life God desires for them. In our polarized, distracted age, it can feel very difficult for Christian leaders to do this. To gain ground requires spiritual exercise, spiritual practice, and spiritual community.

For several years, Jared Boyd has been developing the "Order of Sustainable Faith," a missional monastic expression for the Vineyard Movement, which will be united first by this Rule of Life. Winsome, humble, and wise beyond his years, Jared is showing the way that there are deep affinities between the instincts of the Vineyard and the instincts of Christian monastics, ancient and modern. Neither faddish nor self-aggrandizing, Boyd's "Order of Sustainable Faith" provides a way for Vineyard leaders to practice becoming both/and active contemplatives. We will do well to listen to what he has to say, to participate with him for our own good, and to partner with him for the good of future generations of Vineyard leaders.

— *Caleb Maskell, Society of Vineyard Scholars*

Whether considering a monastic vocation as outlined in these pages, or simply seeking to embrace monastic spiritual practices, this short rule is a treasure. As a Pastor, this rule outlines several practices that are already enhancing my ability to lead a congregation in the pursuit of Christ. The Contemplative and the Missional are interwoven in such a way to empower communities and individuals to practice generosity, simplicity, and reconciliation. Jared has fully embraced John Wimber's admonition to "Take the best and leave the rest" as he has mined the rich heritage and practices of monastic spiritual traditions— actively embodying the ministry of reconciliation that this rule advocates.

— *Jeff Cannell, Pastor/Church Planter*

One of the joys and challenges of being a part of the Vineyard is to maintain a heart of openness and receptivity to the promptings of the Holy Spirit. This can seem a simple matter when those promptings fit within the framework of what we are used to and comfortable with. When the nudging of the Spirit beckons us to step outside of familiar boundaries and structures, we often find resistance welling up in our hearts. But the Spirit "blows where it wants to, and you hear the sound it makes, but you don't know where it's coming from or where it's going to." Over the last few years the Spirit has been beckoning Jared Boyd and his family to establish a monastic expression within the Vineyard. I applaud the courage and sensitivity that Jared is showing as he follows the Spirits lead in this new venture, and I look forward to seeing how The Order of Sustainable Faith will broaden and enrich the kingdom ministry of the Vineyard.

-- *Steve Summerell, Spiritual Formation Director for Vineyard Institute*

Spiritual Direction has formed me more into the image of Jesus as I have tried to navigate living faithfully to Him, while leading in the midst of a frenetic, distracted, and individualistic culture. As a spiritual director in the Vineyard, I have witnessed people encounter the voice of the Spirit, not just in a moment—but over a period of time. The Order of Sustainable Faith is working to highlight this work as a central intention for the life of leaders—to allow an honest space where they can pay attention to the work that the Father is already doing within them, and in the world around them. This missional expression of monasticism encourages the tension between action and adoration in one's life with God. I think it will help leaders to reproduce what is virtuous— enabling us to lead and serve until we meet Jesus face to face.

-- *Sara Carlisle, Spiritual Director*

TABLE OF CONTENTS

1.0

THE VISION & MISSION OF THE ORDER OF SUSTAINABLE FAITH

1.1.0 BASIC VISION

The Order of Sustainable Faith is the membership of those who, with the counsel of a Spiritual Director or Pastor, have responded to this *invitation* and have committed a season of their life to living under these shared *commitments*. The Order will be composed of members (residential, domestic, and non-residential) seeking to live out this *Rule of Life* in dialogue with a Spiritual Director.

1.2.0 MONASTIC

The Order of Sustainable Faith is a distinctly *monastic* expression committed to the work of the Kingdom of God. Historically, monasticism has taken the form of mendicant orders (Franciscans, Jesuits, Dominicans) and cloistered orders (Benedictines, Cistercians, Carmelites). We seek to take the best of both of these traditions and embody what we can of each, as the Spirit leads, and as we discern together his leading.

1.2.1   The Non-Residential Expression will seek to live into a way of life modeled after the mendicant orders. These members will continue to live in their own place of residence while pursuing spiritual direction with this *Rule of Life* as a basis for conversation.

1.2.2   Non-Residential Members may choose to be *placed* at a particular location or city as part of an invitation to participate in a *12-month-mission* (see § 3.5.13).

1.2.3   Non-Residential Membership is meant to express the desire for mobility and the willingness to go anywhere in response to God's invitation.

1.2.4   Residential Members will seek to live into a way and rhythm of life modeled after the cloistered orders. Members will live together in shared living quarters with each individual engaging in a rhythm of work, prayer, sabbath, and study. This *rule of life* will be a guide for conversation with a spiritual director while living in an intentional community with others during a specified period of time.

1.2.5   The Residential Expression is meant to express the desire and willingness to practice stability, in response to God's invitation.

1.2.6   Domestic Members will live closely aligned with the work and community of a specific Residential Expression, but not necessarily in shared housing.

1.2.7   The Domestic Expression will seek to blend together the Non-Residential and Residential Expressions.

1.2.8   All expressions will live the *Rule of Life* in a rhythm that seeks to nurture flourishing in silence, solitude, and a deep engagement with the work and institution of the church.

1.3.0   INTEGRATED

Our life together will seek the integration of singles, couples, families, and those who have chosen a celibate life. No form of living is to be regarded as greater or lesser. In each way of living there is an invitation to seek after God in the *consecrated life.*

1.3.1   Each family dwelling will be considered its own monastic cell with the family unit inhabiting its own space and creating an environment of simplicity, playfulness, care, and education, as each family sees fit.

1.3.2   In Residential Communities:

- Singles will be provided with a cell for living and study.
- Married couples will share one enlarged cell for living and study.
- Families will be provided an appropriate dwelling for the family.
- Communal space will be provided for all in the Residential Community. This space will always be open to guests.

1.3.3   Families may also choose to share housing with non-family members as they feel led.

1.4.0   THE MISSION OF THE ORDER

The Order of Sustainable Faith exists to provide solidarity as well as a small degree of unanimity among those within the Vineyard Movement who desire to move more deeply into the *contemplative life* and who desire to do so in conversation with a Spiritual Director, with guidance from this *rule of life.*

1.4.1   This Order will serve as a support to those seeking a clarity in one's *vocational call* and/or *charism* in the Kingdom of God. (see § 6.1) Once clarity of *vocation & charism* is discerned by a member, the Order will serve as a resource to those actively pursuing a missional life. It is our desire to nurture courageous people into the contemplative and active life.

1.4.2   We desire to serve the larger Vineyard Movement by fostering an ongoing commitment to spiritual formation and spiritual direction.

1.4.3   We desire to plant Residential Communities that will work toward deepening our connection with historic *monasticism* and the commitments contained in this *Rule of Life.*

1.5.0   THE RULE OF LIFE

This *Rule of Life* is meant to provide a basis for the intentional cultivation of ones' discernment toward *vocation and charism* in the work of the kingdom of God.

1.5.1   Let this *Rule of Life* be the base upon which Members may build a deeper sense of *invitation* and one's own set of *commitments.* This process of moving from the general to the specifics of one's life will be a creative and ongoing process, in community and prayer, through struggle and consolations, and always through the guidance of the Holy Spirit.

1.5.2   This *Rule of Life* may be added to by each Residential Community wishing to join The Order of Sustainable Faith. As with any monastic order, no two communities will look alike, and each will take on their own preferences and particularities. Changes to the *Rule of Life* by each community can be made through conversation and discernment alongside the Steering Community of The Order.

1.5.3   It is to be expected that one's way of living this *Rule* will change over time as an individual's life and community moves through seasons. The basic structure of this *Rule* is meant to provide contexts for ongoing reflection and self-awareness regarding each area of the *Rule*. What we will share in common is a deep engagement in discerning how each of these commitments are lived out in the particularity of one's own life. Our lives, and conversations, will shape one another.

2.0

OUR STRUCTURE OF LEADERSHIP

2.1.0   THE OFFICES

The Director of the Order, the Lead Spiritual Director, and the Director of Learning are the only offices held in The Order of Sustainable Faith. We will pursue a model of shared leadership, each operating according to his/her gifts. All other offices are held in each residential community.

2.2.0   THE DIRECTOR

The Director will serve The Order by providing leadership of non-residential members in collaboration with an appointed Lead Spiritual Director and Director of Learning.

2.2.1   The Director will serve The Order by providing leadership to the planting of new Residential Communities in collaboration with the Steering Community of The Order.

2.2.2   The Order of Sustainable Faith will be led by a Director who is appointed through a process of prayer and discernment and in collaboration with regional and national Vineyard pastors and leaders.

2.2.3   The Director of The Order will serve in submission to the regional and national leadership of Vineyard USA.

2.3.0   THE LEAD SPIRITUAL DIRECTOR

The Lead Spiritual Director will oversee the training and development of a network of Spiritual Directors that may serve both as Members of The Order and as Spiritual Directors within The Order.

2.3.1   Spiritual Directors within The Order provide spiritual direction to Residential, Domestic, and Non-Residential Members.

2.3.2   The Lead Spiritual Director will be appointed through a process of prayer and discernment by the Steering Community.

2.4.0   THE DIRECTOR OF LEARNING

The Director of Learning will oversee educational consultation and coaching for Members who are developing a plan of study. Additionally, The Director of Learning will actively seek partnership with resources for education and equipping.

2.4.1   The Director of Learning will be appointed through a process of prayer and discernment by the Steering Community.

2.5.0   THE ADVISORY BOARD

An Advisory Board will be in place for the purpose of discernment and care for the offices of The Order of Sustainable Faith and for the financial health of The Order. The Advisory Board will be made up of 6-10 people chosen by the Director, the Lead Spiritual Director, and the Director of Learning. The Advisory Board will meet quarterly, either in person or with the aid of video technology.[5]

2.6.0   THE STEERING COMMUNITY

A Steering Community will be in place for the purpose of discernment in setting the direction of future plans for The Order and practical considerations of vocational work of The Order. The Steering Community will consist of appointed members of The Order and representatives of other Vineyard ecclesial bodies who have been invited into partnership at this level.

2.6.1   Each Residential Community of The Order of Sustainable Faith will assign a member from their community to join the Steering Community of The Order. The Steering Community will meet no less than two times per year.[6]

2.6.2   We recognize that the best decisions are made when they are made with a diversity of viewpoints represented. The Order

---

5   For a current list of Advisory Board members please visit our website.

6   For a current list of Steering Committee members please visit our website.

will intentionally welcome the voices of women, racial minorities, and non-western cultures. It is our intention that each of these historically marginalized groups be represented on the Steering Community.

3.0

AN INVITATION TO MEMBERSHIP

3.1.0   MEMBERSHIP
Anyone who wishes to pursue this *Rule of Life* should first seek the input of a pastor and, when possible, be in conversation with a Spiritual Director.

3.1.1   There are three types of membership: Residential, Domestic, and Non-Residential.

3.1.3   Each Member is an equal partner in the The Order of Sustainable Faith.

3.1.4   Membership is open to anyone who is committed to living in alignment with this Rule of Life. Those wishing to pursue membership, through the postulancy process and the novitiate experience, are making a commitment to live in alignment with this Rule of Life. People who identify with the following descriptions are particularly encouraged toward membership:

3.1.5   One who is beginning to sense a vocational call or the desire to clarify one's *charism* for work in the Kingdom of God.

Often, God's invitation to us begins with some small bit of vision or picture of what our life could be based upon the current work that he is doing in and around us. We invite members to live this rule for a season of life to intentionally press into the deep desires of one's heart, the uniqueness of God's creative work in you, and to help you discern where God might be leading you to actively put your hand to work.

3.1.6   One who has discerned a more specific call or charism from God (to plant a church, toward cross-cultural work, to pursue academia, etc.) and would like to live more deeply into a rhythm of life as a preparation for the work ahead.

Grounding one's life in a deep rhythm of prayer and work, solitude and engagement, silence and words, will benefit any leader who is preparing to birth something new. We invite members to live this rule for a season of life to create healthy rhythms, increase their self-awareness, and engage in a course of study in preparation for one's vocation.

3.1.7   One who is in need of some mid-stream clarity in one's vocation or charism.

Perhaps you are sensing a change in your life and are being drawn toward something new. Sometimes there is not enough space to transition out of the work you are in the midst of to the new work to which you feel called. We invite members to live this rule for a season of life, to engage more deeply with a spiritual director, and to listen more closely to your life regarding what might lie ahead. Pastors in need of a sabbatical, leaders on the brink of burn-out, and cross-cultural workers transitioning back home. These are just a few examples of individuals (and/or families) who might be in need of a season of rest and a more focused time of discernment.

3.1.8   One who has lived well for many years into their vocational call.

Pastors and leaders "retire" or simply raise up new leaders, and the influence and audience they once had is entrusted to another; and yet they long to give more. Sometimes, the ability to pass on wisdom exceeds one's ability to maintain an official "role" for doing so. We invite members to live this rule for a season of life, to receive training as a spiritual director, and to participate in nurturing in others a life of deep listening, wisdom, and courage. Within a Residential Expression, The Order will work to free up time for you to write, or teach, or mentor others during these years.

3.1.9   One who is spiritually seeking and would like to consider the teachings of Jesus.

The invitation to experience life with God is always open. The life and the words of Jesus provide plenty of ground for exploration regarding some of the most pressing questions. We invite members to live this rule for a season of life, to engage with the teachings of Jesus in an intentional way in cooperation with a spiritual director, and to join us in a rhythm of life that is designed to create fertile soil for spiritual experiences.

3.2.0 RESIDENTIAL MEMBERSHIP

3.2.1 Residential expressions of The Order will serve as missional monastic communities with a commitment to the stability of the place - the land or neighborhood where they are located - and the people who are present.

3.2.2 Each Residential Community will pursue the following areas of service:

- To serve those who have come for a specified season to build a deeper and more personal rhythm of life in preparation for moving into one's vocational work and charism in the Kingdom of God.
- To serve and nurture life with God for those in the neighborhood and city around the Residential Community.
- To serve those who have come to prepare to birth a new Residential Community of The Order of Sustainable Faith in a new location.
- To serve in the community's shared work and economy.

3.2.3 Residential Members are committed to living in the context of intentional community in a house, collection of houses, or monastery under the leadership of a Residential spiritual director appointed by the Lead spiritual director of The Order.

3.2.4 Singles, Married Couples, and Families can be invited into Residential Membership.

3.2.5   In general, Residential Members commit to residence for a specified period of one to five years.

Special circumstances may permit some flexibility on both sides of this commitment.

3.2.6   Those who have chosen to take a formal vow of life-long membership in The Order of Sustainable Faith may be granted a continued stay by the Residential Community. This continued residency is dependent upon many factors. A life-long vow does not necessarily equate with life-long residential membership. These decisions will be discerned by the Residential Community in collaboration with the member wishing to make formal life-long vows and the Steering Community of The Order.

3.2.7   Each Residential Community will fill the following offices prior to the planting of the community:

- The *Residential Spiritual Director*, trained as a spiritual director, will lead the spiritual life and formation of the community and will facilitate the resourcing of each individual member.
- The *Community Manager* will manage the affairs, both practical and economical of the Residential Community.
- The *Table Manager* will oversee the preparation of food for both Residential Members and guests of the Residential Community in cooperation with the Community Manager.

· A *Hospitality Manger* will oversee the sleeping arrangements and hospitality of both Residential Members and guests of the Residential Community in cooperation with the Community Manager.
· A *Vocational Manger* will oversee the chosen vocational work of the Residential Community (farming, bread-baking, bee-keeping, etc.) in cooperation with the Community Manager.

3.3.0   DOMESTIC MEMBERSHIP

3.3.1   The Domestic Expression recognizes that the most basic unit of community is a family. There are seasons of life when a focus on one's own family unit is of greater importance than a focus on community outside the home.

3.3.2   Domestic Members may share in labor and the economy of a Residential Community. This will be determined on a case-by-case basis through a discernment process set forth by the Residential Community.

3.3.3   Domestic Members can hold offices in a Residential Community.

3.3.4   Domestic Members are committed to living in collaboration with a specific Residential Community. Domestic Members generally live in their own residence with a lesser commitment to intentional community.

3.3.5   There may be circumstances that do not allow for an individual or a couple to participate fully in the life of a Residential Community. The Domestic Membership offers a full invitation to communal life without requiring residency in the community. Domestic Members determine their own level of commitment in collaboration with members of a Residential Community.

3.3.6   Domestic Membership may be extended to singles, married couples, and families.

3.3.7   Housing for Domestic Members is not provided by The Order.

3.4.0   NON-RESIDENTIAL MEMBERSHIP

3.4.1   Non-Residential Members will meet with a spiritual director once a month during *Postulancy* and every three weeks during the *Novitiate Experience* (see § 3.5 for details). This Rule of Life will be the basis for conversations and spiritual direction.

3.4.2   Non-Residential Members should commit to living this *Rule of Life* in their present location and context with the ongoing support of a spiritual director and participation in the life of a local church. When possible, participation in the life of a Residential Community during holiday or vacation is encouraged.

3.4.3   Some Non-Residential Members will be members who have left their most natural mode of life and residence in response to an inner invitation to participate in a *12-month-mission* (see § 3.5.13).

3.5.0   ENTERING INTO MEMBERSHIP

3.5.1   *A Request* for membership in The Order will consist of a discernment process between the applicant and the applicant's spiritual director and/or pastor.[7]

3.5.2   Every member will begin with a 6-month *postulancy* as a Non-Residential Member.

3.5.3   During *postulancy*, members will review the Rule of Life, meet with a spiritual director, and continue to discern one's desire for membership within The Order of Sustainable Faith. Additionally, a posulate will form a Discerning Community (see § 5.6.5).

3.5.4   Upon completion of the 6-month *postulancy*, members may request to continue into the *novitiate experience*. This request can be for Residential, Domestic, or Non-Residential Membership.

3.5.6   Completion of the 6-month *postulancy* is a requirement for entering a Residential Community.

3.5.7   The *novitiate experience* is a commitment of 1 year beyond *postulancy*.

3.5.8   During the novitiate experience, members enter more deeply into a rhythm of life. Novice members, in collaboration with other members and a spiritual director, will be in conversation and discernment toward developing a more specified and individualized Rule of Life.

---

7   For a current overview of the discernment process for The Order of Sustainable Faith, and to receive an Invitation to Membership, please visit: sustainablefaith.com.

3.5.9   The focus for the *novitiate experience* is to pay attention to the *invitation* that comes to you during *postulancy*, and to build upon that invitation.

3.5.10   Upon completion of the 1-year *novitiate experience*, members may, through a discernment process with other members and/or a spiritual director, make a longer commitment to membership within The Order of Sustainable Faith.

3.5.11   Longer commitments are initially an additional 12-42 months beyond the *novitiate experience.* The duration of a longer commitment is at the member's discretion.

3.5.12   At the end of 5 years of membership in The Order (from the beginning of *postulancy*), members may request to make life-long vows.

3.5.13   In making a longer commitment beyond the *novitiate experience*, members may discern whether to commit to a *12-month mission* somewhere in the world. This *mission* will be in collaboration with a Vineyard church-plant, a cross-cultural ministry context alongside Vineyard Missions, or a Residential Community of The Order of Sustainable Faith. This *12-month mission* should be selected because it has a practical focus that aligns with the sense of God's direction in a person's life.

3.5.14   For those not wishing to make life-long vows, Residential Membership is limited to a five-year commitment.

4.0
OUR RHYTHM OF LIFE

4.1.0 BODILY LABOR

In solidarity with monastic life that has gone before us, our rhythm of life engages in bodily labor, prayer, learning, and rest.

4.1.1 Bodily Labor reminds of us the goodness of limits. Our commitment to bodily labor is a commitment to stand in solidarity with monastic communities who have gone before us for whom bodily labor was a necessary part of spiritual formation. Through bodily labor we embrace the weakness of our body and recognize in it God's invitation toward activity and rest.

4.1.2 Residential Members should be prepared to receive a job according to their skill and ability that serves the sustainability of the community. Each job in a Residential Community should support the management of the community directly (food preparation, maintenance), or the chosen vocational work of the community (farming, tending bees, baking bread, making furniture, etc) that serves to support the economy of the community.

4.1.3   Domestic Members will discern together with a Residential Community what bodily labor might be best for the Domestic Member within the Residential Community. Domestic Members with work commitments outside the community will create space for bodily labor within the community.

4.1.4   Non-Residential Members living in close proximity to a Residential Community should be willing to receive a job from the Community Manager that helps support the sustainability of the community, or the chosen vocational work of the community.

4.1.5   Non-Residential Members not living in close proximity to a Residential Community should pursue bodily work by volunteering in a local organization that shares the values of vocational work of The Order and engages in the work of "new creation." This work should be chosen in conversation with a spiritual director.

4.2.0   PRAYER

4.2.1   In Prayer, we cry out to God with thanksgiving for God's kingdom now. We groan for God's future kingdom to come in its fullness.

4.2.2   Our prayers, both individually and communally, are to be entered into always as a space of invitation. A rhythm of prayer for the individual should be discerned in conversation with a spiritual director.

4.2.3   Each member should, in collaboration
         with his or her spiritual director, develop
         a practice of daily examen at mid-day and
         before bed.

4.2.4   Residential Members should meet for
         fixed-hour prayer at hours determined by
         the community under the leadership of
         the community's Spiritual Director. Each
         community should guide their own rhythm
         of praying-the-hours as determined by the
         needs of the community. Each community
         should engage in at least one fixed-hour
         time of prayer together using a liturgy or
         prayer-book chosen by the Spiritual Director.

         Residential Members will also commit to
         intercessory prayer for Domestic Members
         and Non-Residential Members.

4.2.5   Domestic Members will enter into the
         rhythm of prayer alongside the Residential
         Community. Domestic Members will
         commit to intercessory prayer for the
         Residential Community and for Non-
         Residential Members.

4.2.6   Non-Residential Members will develop a
         daily rhythm of prayer in collaboration
         with a Spiritual Director.

         Non-Residential Members will commit
         to intercessory prayer for the Residential
         Communities and for Domestic Members of
         the Order.

4.3.0 STUDY

4.3.1 The practices of study and contemplation form the desires of our heart and reveal the places in this world where our gifts and desires can be given in service. Each member, with the help of the Director of Learning, will develop a course of study that is specific to the member's season of life and reason for entering into The Order.

4.3.2 Each member - Residential, Domestic, and Non-Residential - will set aside time each week for study as part of his/her rule of life.

4.3.3 Some examples of a course of study for a member:

- Enroll in Vineyard Institute
- Enroll in an advanced degree program or vocational training program
- Enroll in an "at-a-distance" program through an accredited institution
- Develop a course of study related to a specific area of ministry to which one feels drawn (for example, a lengthy study of the work of healing and prophetic ministry).

This is not meant to be an exhaustive list, and creativity and discernment are expected.

4.4.0 REST

4.4.1 Each member should pursue an understanding of the value of rest and Sabbath.

4.4.2 Each Residential Community should discern their own needs regarding hours of quiet, periods of silence and Sabbath under the leadership of the Residential Spiritual Director. In light of our current cultural context in which rest and Sabbath are so deficient, rest and Sabbath are to be strictly observed and respected in each community.

4.4.3 Non-Residential Members, in collaboration with a Spiritual Director, should develop a rhythm of rest, sleep, and sabbath that is in spirit with *The Order* and serves to develop one's own formational life.

4.4.4 Domestic Members should also be in conversation with a spiritual director regarding rest and Sabbath. When possible, domestic members should follow the rhythm of rest as discerned by the Residential Community to which they are connected. However, when there are work and commitments outside of the Residential Community, a Domestic Member should also understand that a more specific rule for rest and Sabbath may be needed.

5.0

COMMITMENTS

5.1.0 AN INTRODUCTION TO COMMITMENTS

We make the following commitments not out of compulsion, but out of sensing an invitation from God to move more deeply and with a greater intentionality into both the contemplative and active life. Each of these commitments is to be explored in the context of spiritual direction, and with the aid of resources outside of this rule. We trust that with some prayer and conversation with others, God will invite you into a deeper understanding of each of these commitments within the context of your own life. Additional resources for each of these commitments can be suggested through conversation with other members and with The Order's Director of Learning.

Alongside each commitment is a list of a few questions. These represent the types of questions to consider in the context of spiritual direction and formation.

5.2.0 SPIRITUAL DIRECTION

5.2.1 Spiritual Direction is at the center of the experience of a member in The Order of Sustainable Faith. For every other commitment we are making - be it to align ourselves to this rule of life, or to align ourselves toward something to which the Spirit is leading - *spiritual direction* will provide a context for conversation and discernment.

5.2.2 In Spiritual Direction we are being intentional about our conversation with God. We are looking for themes in our prayer, and listening for God's voice in our life with another person alongside of us.

5.2.3 Our commitment to Spiritual Direction is meant to nurture the conversations we are having with God and our own perception of self - as we really are, not as we wish to be.

5.2.4 · What is the movement of God in my life?
· What is happening in and around me that makes me hopeful?
· What activities in my life are nurturing intimacy with God and a desire to follow Jesus, wherever he may lead?

5.3.0 SILENCE, SOLITUDE, AND THE CONTEMPLATIVE LIFE

5.3.1 In silence, solitude, and the contemplative life there is an invitation to know God and to know ourselves.

5.3.2 We seek silence because we want to hear from God.

5.3.3 We seek solitude because we know that we are attached to so much. In solitude, we find out what (and who) we long for when those things are not present. This longing reveals our attachments and the things that have power over us. We offer these attachments to God and ask that he make our desires rightly ordered.

5.3.4 The contemplative life is lived with the intention and willingness to hear God speak. We cooperate with God's grace and the Holy Spirit in order to be open to hearing whatever it is that God would speak, through the means of our daily lives. In prayer, in silence, in work, and in relationship— God is speaking and inviting us into his great love and into his way. The contemplative life is a life that is listening.

5.3.5 · What is God saying to me when I am silent?
· What do I think about when everything is quiet?
· How do I feel when I am alone?
· Who am I with when I feel most alive to God?

5.4.0 SIMPLICITY AND (WHEN POSSIBLE) POVERTY

5.4.1 Our life together, in both Residential and Non-Residential expressions, pursues simplicity in a world of increasing complexity. Each member, in prayer and leading by the Holy Spirit, and in collaboration with a spiritual director, should develop his/her own way of living that intentionally moves toward greater simplicity.

5.4.2   As with any formational practices and commitments that are counter-cultural, these are to be pursued with humility and without judgment of others.

5.4.3   We invite members to consider the following areas as contexts where the pursuit of simplicity may come into focus. We choose simplicity not for the sake of simplicity, but for formation of our own lives and the way they are "lived" in the world.

5.4.4   **Clothing**
Clothing can often be an expression of individuality and a creative outlet for beauty. This can be celebrated and even nurtured. However, it also can be a context for some degree of obsession regarding the latest fashion - feeding a need to "fit in." We seek to hold these expressions in tension.

5.4.5   While we do not share a common wardrobe or dictate a "style" of clothing for members, we invite members to consider how their choice of clothing is reflective of their life with God. For example, some may choose to invest in a few items of clothing, manufactured in a way that honors life and is not dependent upon slave-labor. Others may find that choosing clothes at a thrift-store - an approach that "reuses what has not been used up" - allows for a wider variety. In our choice of clothing, we are trying to combat an attitude of *consumption.*

5.4.6   Our commitment is toward a deep consideration of how our purchase of clothing impacts individuals and cultures that are currently being exploited for cheap labor, often in conditions where injustice reigns.

5.4.7
· Am I willing to stand against systems of injustice when it is inconvenient for me?
· Am I content with what I look like? With my body? Why or Why not?

5.4.8 In pursuit of a life of simplicity, the invitation is toward less, not more.

5.4.9 **Food**
Our relationship with food, as a culture, is in remarkable trouble. Our commitment to simplicity in eating supports our care for our bodies and also supports our commitment to a healthy agricultural system. We invite members to take great interest in what and how they eat, recognizing that what we put into our bodies is often reflected in our emotional life and well-being.

5.4.10 Residential Members will find that meals are simple, but wholesome, well-prepared, but not meant to impress. Where possible, we will use what we can produce, and buy what we need from nearby sources.

5.4.11 Non-Residential Members will be encouraged to dialogue with a spiritual director about food, eating and fasting, and the role of food in spiritual formation.

5.4.12
· How are periods of "fasting" and periods of "feasting" a part of my spiritual formation?
· What happens to me when I remove food from my life for a period of time?

· What happens to me when I celebrate through feasting and abundance?

5.4.13 Each Residential Community will develop its own rhythm of "fasting and feasting" in collaboration with the Director and Lead Spiritual Director.

5.4.14 **Possessions**
Possessions, the things we have and keep, are often a reflection of cultural values and not necessarily neutral in their effect on our lives. In a western consumer culture, it is often not the possession itself (some new gadget or a smarter phone) that meets a great need, but its acquisition.

5.4.15 Our commitment to simplicity for what we own and keep will not categorically label certain types of possessions to be avoided and others to be embraced. But rather, simplicity regarding possessions will be a consideration in the context of Spiritual Direction and under guidance by the Holy Spirit. We invite members to look deeply at what forces are at work that lead one to want something he/she currently does not have. Through consistent examen and reflection we trust that through the work of the Holy Spirit, any *disordered attachment*[8] to ownership will be revealed in a member's life.

8   *Disordered attachments* is a concept found in Ignatian Spirituality, and, more specifically, in the Spiritual Exercises of Ignatius. Ignatius believed that disordered (or inordinate) attachments are rooted in a desire for riches, honor, and pride. The Exercises, along with a daily examination of conscience, help in paying attention to areas of one's life that may be preventing total freedom in following Jesus.

5.4.16 · How are the things we have or want getting in the way of following Jesus?
· Is there currently any possession I am longing for? Is there anything else behind the longing for this possession?

5.4.17 It will be assumed that Residential members will have downsized in order to come to live in a Residential Community. Practically, the *footprint* of one's room will by itself radically limit the possessions one may bring into a Residential Community.

5.4.18 **Technology**
Technology is not to be regarded as good or bad. A great deal of technology allows for *life*, while some life is choked out by our gadgets and our addiction to them. Our commitment to simplicity carries with it a commitment to open-handedness with our engagement with technology.

5.4.19 We seek to be *indifferent*[9] to the role that this dominant feature of our current culture plays in our life. We are not striving to be counter-cultural simply for the sake of standing against the prevalent culture. However, we recognize simply that our relationship with technology is often not a *neutral* relationship. The effects of

9 This too is a concept from Ignatius. At the beginning of the Spiritual Exercises, Ignatius writes that "we ought not to seek health rather than sickness, wealth rather than poverty, honor rather than dishonor, a long life rather than a short one." We mention it here in relation to technology because technology is often laden with the narrative that it gives us exactly what we want. Indifference means a healthy sense of faith that whatever circumstances I may be in—it's okay, God's in it somewhere.

social media, for example, are still not entirely understood. We aim to engage in conversations that seriously consider what is or isn't best for our personal life and relationships. As in other areas, here there is no hard and fast rule but an invitation toward responding to God through an intentional *examen* of our current practice.

5.4.20 · Where is my relationship with technology creating complexity in my life and relationships?

5.4.21 **Poverty**
In some contexts, members may feel an invitation toward voluntary poverty. Poverty is not regarded as more *spiritual*, though for some, a season of intentional poverty may be a path toward a deeper formation. We wish to arrive at a place where we are seeking neither to give up our possessions nor to retain them unless directed by God through prayer and affirmed in community. There are contexts even outside the church where individuals choose poverty as an act of solidarity with the poor and to better understand the plight of those who have little.

5.4.22 We are open to God's invitation toward voluntary poverty recognizing that we could give away all our possessions to the poor - and yet if we do not have *love*, we gain nothing. We view poverty as one area that God might extend his invitation to me in my current context.

5.4.23   · Would a season of intentional poverty help free me up in some way in my life with God?

5.4.24   Decisions for individuals to move toward voluntary poverty will be discerned in each community. Members wishing to enter into a season of voluntary poverty will first present the desire to their spiritual director who will help them in furthering the conversation with those around them.

5.4.25   Members with families, particularly those with children, will be strongly encouraged to take a form of voluntary poverty that does not allow one's invitation toward poverty to adversely effect one's responsibilities to provide for one's family.

5.5.0   CHASTITY

5.5.1   The historical commitment for monastic communities has been *chastity*. While the apostle Paul spoke of the *gift* of singleness, celibacy has often been overemphasized as a thing to be pursued rather than as a gift to be nurtured. We seek to hold both marriage and singleness in celebration and to see true *celibacy* found in each expression.

5.5.2   We are committed to nurturing singleness to whom it has been given as a gift. Devotion to one's *charism* and/or vocation in the work of building God's Kingdom, apart from the concerns of marriage and family, is clearly a model that has demonstrated the Spirit of God at work throughout history. In spiritual direction, singles will find space for conversation regarding one's call toward either singleness or marriage. The single life is a celibate life.

5.5.3
- Where is God's invitation to me in my singleness?
- Do I sense *struggle* or *grace* during this season of singleness?
- If I find a desire for a life-long partner during this time of singleness, where does the desire stem from?

5.5.4   We are committed to nurturing marriages. For those whom God has invited into a marriage relationship, it is also a place where God's grace and Spirit are working. In marriage, one is committed to another, as an expression and demonstration of Christ's love for the church as well as an expression of love and companionship. In spiritual direction, those engaged in the married life will be looking for ways that God is speaking through one's life-long partner. The invitation here is to pay attention.

5.5.5
- Where do I find life in serving my partner?
- How is God loving me through this other person? How am I being challenged?
- Where do I find resistance in this relationship?

5.5.6   We are committed to nurturing the sexual life and sexual expression in the context of a life-long commitment alone.

5.5.7   For singles, *celibacy* means sexual abstinence.

5.5.8 For married couples, *celibacy* means sexual faithfulness to one's life-long partner.

· How is God at work in my sexuality?

5.6.0 OBEDIENCE IN THE CONTEXT OF A DISCERNING COMMUNITY

Obedience is one of the three main vows of historic monastic communities (poverty, chastity, and *obedience*). In keeping with this tradition, and with a recognition that the contemplative life is a life that moves toward greater humility, we invite members to commit to *obedience* in the context of a discerning community.

5.6.1 Obedience to the Holy Spirit

We believe that God is speaking through His Holy Spirit in a variety of ways. We are committed to an intentional listening to God's invitation in our lives and acting upon that invitation, whatever the cost. We commit to vulnerability and honesty in our close relationships, recognizing that God's invitation to us often comes through the voice of another person. Our commitment to obedience is a commitment to not ignoring God's command and invitation when it comes to us. Vulnerability is necessary if we are to discern God's voice and leading.

5.6.2 · What is God currently asking of me? What RISK is he currently setting before me?
· What is God asking me to do? What am I doing to respond to God's leading?
· Am I being honest?

· Am I confronting what is before me?

5.6.4 **Obedience within a Discerning Community**
There are times when decisions are risky or weighty. There are also times when change is necessary, and costly. We are committed to standing against the spirit of autonomy. We are committed to Community. Christ gave us an example of humility when he put his hands into the life of others. A vow of obedience in our context is a vow that is meant to create freedom and faith in making decisions and navigating one's life with God.

5.6.5 Each member, upon entering into *postulancy*, will choose 5 or 6 individuals who will make up a designated *Discerning Community*. This group will be made up of a combination of members of The Order and non-members, and may include one's spiritual director.

5.6.6 On occasions when a member would like to receive input regarding a decision, or, when a member feels stuck in one's life with God, a clearness committee can be called by the member during which the member's *Discerning Community* will gather together to help the member.[10]

5.6.7 Members may also present an issue to one's *Discerning Community*, and, through discernment and in conversation with one's spiritual director, may request that

---

10 The Clearness Committee is a method of communal discernment developed by the Quakers. More information and training in this practice are available upon request.

the *Discerning Community* serve in the role of "Superior" regarding the issue at hand. In short, a member can choose obedience to a decision made by one's *discerning community*.

5.6.8 In this way, we allow for the work of relinquishing control. We invite others to speak into our lives, to listen intently, and to discern together what God's best for us might be. By giving others permission to make decisions for our life, in the context of friendship and love, we are getting at the heart of humility.

5.6.9 It would be a rare occasion that one's discerning community would decide against the expressed desires of the individual member. If one has reached a point in prayer that would allow such a relinquishment of control, it is likely that one's desires are in the right place, and well-informed.

5.6.10 It is not the outcome that is most important, but the process. The commitment toward a willingness to obey in this way makes room for God to be at work.

- Am I willing to let others make this decision for me? Do I trust my community? Do I trust that God can speak in a significant way through others?
- What resistance is there to placing this decision into another's hand?
- Am I willing to hear "No" to my current question? Am I willing to hear, "Yes"?

5.7.0 SHARED WORK

5.7.1 Residential Communities will share work together. Each Residential Community will determine the kind of vocational work to be shared that will allow the community to eventually be self-sustaining through the production of products or the offering of services to the community surrounding the Residential Community.

5.7.2 The chosen work should keep in mind the commitment to *bodily labor* (see § 4.1) and engage in cultural formation and craftsmanship.

5.7.3 Domestic Members and Non-Residential Members who live near a Residential Expression should also be prepared to share in the vocational work.

5.7.4 · What is God revealing to me in the work I contribute to the community?
· Where do I find life in the work of our community? What am I drawn to?
· What feels difficult about the work we share together?

5.8.0 SHARED ECONOMY

5.8.1 We seek to nurture an economy of *giving* and *generosity*. To that end, our *economy* is shared among members of all expressions. While we will not have a *shared purse* entirely, we are committed to meeting the needs of members in The Order as well as those in need throughout the world. Each member should think of his or her possessions as belonging to the Lord.

5.8.2   Through Spiritual Direction and in listening to the Holy Spirit, we will make our needs known to each other, and we will trust God to meet those needs.

5.8.3   Each Residential Community will manage its own economy while seeking to help other Residential Communities who might be in need.

5.8.4   · Where do I sense God's invitation toward giving?
· Do I currently see any practical needs around me in my community?
· Are there any assets I might have that could be offered as a gift to someone else? To the community? To the poor?
· Am I growing in generosity?

5.9.0   HOSPITALITY

5.9.1   We seek to regain the ancient spirit and practice of *hospitality* as a marker of Christian obedience and devotion. The practice of welcoming the poor, the stranger, and the pilgrim is a deep practice within the historic church, and most notably in monastic communities.

5.9.2   Residential Communities will welcome all who come for rest and direction, regardless of social status and/or ability to pay for accommodations and food.

5.9.3   The boundaries involved in hospitality can often be difficult to navigate. Each Residential Community will discern together the particulars of *how* they will participate in the practice of hospitality.

5.9.3   We will foster in each member a hospitality of *presence*. Sitting with another, face-to-face, in an unhurried way is a deeply loving act. In relationships, we will seek to eradicate the sense of *hurry* that is so prevalent in our cultural context.

5.9.4   Non-Residential Members should examine their practice of hospitality around opening their home to guests and neighbors, as well as the practice of presence and conversation. One's commitment to hospitality will also require a developing awareness of one's chief motivations and desires regarding the practice of hospitality. These motivations and desires will be explored through spiritual direction.

5.9.5   Members of The Order will intentionally pursue the practice of hospitality toward those of races and ethnicities different from their own. This intentionality is meant to push back against our natural tendency toward racial division.[11]

5.9.6   · What is my posture and attitude toward the stranger? What is my attitude toward those of a different race/ethnicity?
        · When I am with people, am I fully present? What distracts me?
        · Is my home a place of welcome to others? Am I interruptible?
        · Where do I sense hurry in my interactions with people? Where is God's invitation to me toward patience?

---

11 Cleveland, Christena. *Disunity in Christ: uncovering the hidden forces that keep us apart.* IVP press 2013.

- Are there any false motivations in my desire to spend time with people? Am I brokering for power? Influence? Affirmation?
- Where do I see the face of Christ in the needs of others? How do these experiences shape me?

5.10.0 RESTORATIVE PEACEMAKING

5.10.1 *Restorative Peacemaking* is the intentional act of creating a culture of forgiveness.

5.10.2 Conflict will be seen as an opportunity for humility, growth, and intimacy. We will assist one another in the process of moving from *reaction* to *response*, from *self-justification* to *self-reflection*, from *antagonism* to *friendship*. We pursue reconciliation and understanding by being emotionally honest, creating space for our diversity, and honoring each other's gifts and talents.

5.10.3 Trust will be developed through vulnerability and transparency.

5.10.4 We value peacemaking and the process toward humility that is required to live at peace with those whom with we live, and work, and love. We will purse peace with those with whom we are in conflict.

5.10.5 Members of The Order will actively seek to bring restorative peace among those of different races and cultural heritage.

5.10.6 Both *Residential* and *Non-Residential* members will participate in, as part of their rhythm of study, some prepared exercises that relate to *restorative peacemaking.*

5.10.7   When conflict arises between members it should be addressed according to the teachings of Jesus in Matthew 18.

5.10.8   · Are there conflicts that I am currently avoiding?
          · Are there relationships that are currently strained as a result of my own brokenness?
          · Am I being intentional about being vulnerable and transparent about my faults?
          · Am I harboring any judgments or bitterness toward others?

5.11.0   THE EXPRESSION OF FAULTS AND ADMIRATIONS

5.11.1   As part of our rhythm of life, members of The Order are committed to expressing (out loud) their own faults and affirmations of others. In any given week, our failures—our sins against God and against each other—are often not given a proper confession. Likewise, we are not accustomed to speaking out loud the things we notice that God is doing in and through others.

5.11.2   Residential Communities will set aside time each week for *faults and affirmations*—a meeting where *faults* of the past week (or longer) may be confessed, and *affirmations* of others is given proper space. A meeting for faults and affirmations is not to be obligatory. Any member of The Order is welcome to participate, or not.

5.11.3   Faults are to be spoken about oneself.
Affirmations are spoken about others.

5.11.4   **Faults**
When sharing faults, we are mindful of
their appropriateness before bringing them
out in public. In general, faults and sins
which occurred in the open, or ones that
affect the community, are ones that are
appropriate to share in a meeting of *faults
and affirmations.* Private sins should be shared
in private, with a friend or mentor that can
serve to hear one's *confession.*[12]

5.11.5   · "I've noticed this week that I have been
impatient with many of you. Please
forgive me."
· "I've noticed over the past few weeks
that I have been too much in a hurry,
and I haven't taken time to really listen
to others in conversation."
· "Some of you may have heard me speak
unkindly to John yesterday morning at
breakfast. I have already asked for John's
forgiveness—but I understand that my
unkind words affected the mood at
breakfast. Please forgive me."

5.11.6   **Affirmations**
When sharing *affirmations,* we are working
to speak about a specific moment where
we saw God's grace at work in another's
life. This is meant to encourage each other
toward the growth in love, kindness,
humility, and generosity.

---

12   James 5:16

5.11.7 · "Mark, I am grateful for your extra work this week. I can tell that you are looking for ways to serve, and this has been encouraging to me."

· "Josh and Samantha— when you were having conflict yesterday, I noticed that you both spoke patiently and kindly to one another. You were both respectful and showed love to each other. Thank you for this."

5.11.8 *Non-Residential Members* should work toward implementing a time of *faults and affirmations* with roommates, housemates, and/or family members. Other members of The Order will be available to help encourage you to lead in this area within your present context of life.

5.12.0 THE THEOLOGY AND PRACTICE OF THE KINGDOM OF GOD

5.12.1 A commitment to the theology and practice of the kingdom of God is the most fundamental core value in the Vineyard. As part of our place within the Vineyard, The Order of Sustainable Faith will also have this as a core and guiding value. We view the kingdom of God (God's rule and reign with Jesus as King) as the overarching and integrating theme throughout the Bible.

5.12.2 God's mission to the world (*missio dei*) is also our mission to the world. We join God in the work of nurturing life in this world, partnering with God to bring all things under the rule and reign of Jesus.

Participation in the *missio dei* will take on many forms according to each individual's gift and calling.

5.12.3 Our commitment to the *missio dei* and to the practice of *the kingdom* is a commitment to get our hands dirty and create space for God's kingdom to break into the here and now.

5.12.5 We are committed to praying for the sick.

5.12.4 We are committed to prophetic ministry.

5.12.6 We are committed to the *experience of God* in worship: in communal prayer, in silence, and in song.

5.12.7 We are committed to work that shows mercy to the poor.

5.12.8 We are committed to working toward eradicating systemic poverty, which we see as a work toward *justice*.

5.12.9 We are committed to missions (see § 3.5.13).

5.12.9 *Residential Members* of The Order will discern together as a community how to best participate in the *praxis* of the kingdom of God.

5.12.10 *Non-Residential Members* of The Order should live into these commitments in the context of a local church and/or with the support of others.

5.12.11 The theology and practice of the kingdom of God will inform our journey in *spiritual direction* and *formation*.

· What work am I currently most feeling drawn toward?

- Where have I noticed God at work? When have I felt the invitation to join Him in it?
- Am I currently feeling any resistance to step out in any specific area?
- What does my experience of worship feel like right now?
- What is happening in my life that is leading toward experiencing more of God?

5.13.0 IN SERVICE AND SUBMISSION TO THE CHURCH

5.13.1 We are committed to be in service and submission to the church.

5.13.2 The Order of Sustainable Faith will come under the appropriate authority structure, both nationally and regionally, as determined by the current leadership of Vineyard USA.

5.13.3 The Order of Sustainable Faith sees itself as a Missional Monastic Expression planted under the leadership and guidance of Vineyard USA, as a part of the efforts to *multiply healthy communities* within the Vineyard.

6.0
APPENDICES

What follows are some brief investigations of some of the recurring terms and concepts that are woven throughout this Rule. These are not meant to be exhaustive, nor are they meant to be "the final word" on any of these ideas. They are meant to be the beginning of conversations in the context of community.

6.1 ON VOCATION & CHARISM

jared patrick boyd

Throughout this *Rule of Life* we use two words that require some explanation in order to fully understand the nature of our mission and purpose as a religious order situated in the contemplative stream of Christian tradition: vocation *and* charism. I briefly make some definitions below. However, a more robust dialogue on the nature of vocation and charism is warranted, and it is my hope that many conversations will follow this writing.

VOCATION

For the most part, those in the Protestant church since the Reformation have assumed a *vocational* model of work, one that emphasizes a sense of being *called* to a certain task or mission. Both Luther and Calvin articulated a *vocational* view of work, though it was Luther who originated the idea of *vocation*. By the time of Luther, the only understanding of the term *vocation* was a call toward religious life— and more specifically, the monastic life. Luther protested against the concept of higher and lower callings, an idea that was prevalent in the Roman church at the time and was the basis for entering into a monastery. Luther's polemic against monasticism hinged on a translation decision in 1 Corinthians 7:20. Luther translated the Greek term *klesis* (which means *calling*) here, and only here, with a German word *Beruf*, which carried with it more of an external connotation, rather than the sense of an interior *call* of God toward Christ. That our understanding, and often our longing for a deeper sense of hearing God's *call* on our life rests on a translation decision by Luther, is a fact that is fruitful to untangle. Luther's Reformation, in many ways, came out of his own experience of dissatisfaction with the *religious life*. There is a general agreement in Luther's fight against a two-tiered Christianity of monastics and non-monastics), but the implications of Luther's work on the concept of *vocation* has left a mark. [13]

Luther came to hold two beliefs regarding *vocation:* (1) all Christians - not only those called to the monastic life -have a vocation, and (2) *every type of work* performed by Christians can be a vocation. [14] The value of one's work is found in the reality of God's call to the work being performed, regardless of the sphere of life in which it is engaged, religious, or otherwise. The Christian colloquial language that runs something like, "What do you feel God calling you to do?"— this is language with roots in Luther, and, more broadly speaking, Luther's critique of the contemplative (and monastic) way of life. Luther gave theological permission to the everyday person engaged in baking bread and managing a shop, to do so in the service of God. [15]

---

13 Froehlich, Karl. "Luther on Vocation." *Lutheran Quarterly* 13: 195-207.

14 Volf, Miroslav. *Work in the Spirit: toward a theology of work.* Eugene, OR: Wipf and Stock, 2001. p. 105

15 Moltmann, Ju. *On human dignity: political theology and ethics.* Philadelphia: Fortress Press, 1984. p. 47

Miroslov Volf, among others, have offered an important critique of Luther's notion of vocation.[16] Any attempt at developing a consistent theology of work will need to address our current context of work— one that is mobile, industrial, and informational— as well as the alienation that many feel while attempting to discern *the call of God* toward a particular sphere of employment or larger vision for one's life. Additionally, the nature of work in our current cultural context often stands in opposition to our desire to see God's kingdom at work in the world. How does one experience a sense of co-laboring with God when one's work is enmeshed in problematic structures of power, as our work so often is? How do we see God's kingdom moving forward when our place of employment participates in socially and environmentally destructive practices?

Our use of the word *vocation* in this *Rule* is meant to consciously draw attention to our longing to hear *the call* of God on our lives. As inadequate as it is, Luther's notion of vocation is so much a part of our Christian consciousness and church life, that to abandon it altogether would fail to speak to the reality of our experience as it is. To abandon the language of *vocation* due to its inability to fully make sense of our complex relationship with work and finding our place in the world, seems to miss the point. Our expectation for our work to be *more fulfilling* is perhaps an expectation that needs to be explored, but it is nonetheless present.

16 Volf, *Work in the Spirit: toward a theology of work.*, pp. 105-109

The Order of Sustainable Faith is deeply interested in helping to facilitate people hearing and discerning *the call* of God— *the invitation of God*— for their lives. However, we don't take the call of God to be only about the kind of work one does, but also about the particular grace and energy with which to do it. Certainly God's invitation comes to us to more deeply engage in a particular work, with specific people and places. The challenge to hearing this invitation is often wrapped up in *trying* to hear it, rather than simply living out of the grace and energy already present in our lives. The call of God— his invitation toward more— comes as we are faithful with the grace already present. Whatever sense of *vocation* that comes, it seems to come on the tail end of recognizing and operating with the gifts of the Spirit— the *charisms* of God. We find the *call* of God by nurturing what he has already given.

CHARISM

A theology of *charism* is a more helpful foundation as we consider what it means to work with God in the project of transforming the world into *new creation*. Again, Miroslav Volf has informed our view of work and mission:

Charism is not just a call by which God bids us to perform a particular task, but is also an inspiration and a gifting to accomplish the task...the enabling depends on the presence and activity of the Spirit. When people work exhibiting the values of the new creation (as expressed in what Paul calls the "fruit of the Spirit") then the Spirit works in them and through them.[17]

Our aim in extending an invitation for some to more deeply discern their *charism* for work in the kingdom of God is an invitation toward paying closer attention, for a season, to the activity of the Spirit and the energy that comes with it for taking new steps of faith. *Charisms* are gifts given to each person by the Holy Spirit for specific tasks and functions in the world.

Every follower of Jesus is given *charisms*. Every part of the body of Christ has a function, and thus, every person is *gifted* in some way both for the edification of the body and the work of God in the world. Where is the fingerprint of God in your life? Where do you sense the most grace to cooperate with God for what he is doing in the world? We trust that the answers to these questions come over time, with some reflection and paying attention, and often with the help of a spiritual director and a community of people who can *see* things that you can't see. They call out what is in you, not because they need you to do something for them, but because the gift of God - your *charism* - is leaking out of your life; they can't help but help you name it.

One of the greatest drawbacks to a focus on *vocation* is the nature of how our work changes through time. There may be an extended period of grace and gifting for cross-cultural work, but this isn't necessarily a gifting that is irrevocable (see Romans 11:29). The Spirit of God imparts charisms "as he

---

17   Volf, *Work in the Spirit: toward a theology of work.*, p. 114

wills" (1 Corinthians 12:11). Our effort to create space for a deep discernment of *charism*, is to take seriously the movement of God's Spirit in people's lives. Sometimes we finish the task appointed us during a season; what comes next is yet to be known, and the space to truly *know*, it is often limited and hurried. The Order of Sustainable Faith aims to cultivate that space— space in people's lives, physical space in our *Residential Expressions*, and in conversation with a spiritual director.

6.2 ON FAULTS AND AFFIRMATIONS

Evan B. Howard

There is a point in Rumer Godden's novel of monastic life, In This House of Brede, where the nuns comment on their "Chapter of Faults," a gathering for mutual confession. Godden writes, "The Chapter of Faults had the effect of welding the nuns together and making them like one another. "You can't be afraid of someone, even as sharp and clever as Dame Agnes," said Cecily, "when you have seen her kneel down before us all, even us young ones she teaches, and say, 'Three times yesterday I said things that cut,' or 'I lost my temper.'"

"Especially when you know you will probably lose your's tomorrow," said Hilary. (Rumer Godden, In This House of Brede [NY: Viking Press, 1969], 171).

For others, however, their experience of the Chapter of Faults was not so pleasant. One "SARAH" tells of her experience in Marie Thérèse Gass' *Unconventional Women: 73 Ex-Nuns Tell Their Stories*: "Every other Friday night we each knelt in front of the Novice Mistress and confessed a fault, then any of the other 60-90 Novitiate members could stand up and tell us our faults. This was probably the most psychologically damaging process in the Novitiate/Juniorate. It was unhealthy psychologically and built up much resentment among the Sisters." (see pp. 108-115 for this and other stories about Chapter of Faults).

I am thrilled at the development of--and have been consequently concerned for the health of--the many new religious communities springing up.

It is a joy to witness the emergence of courageous communities of Christian believers dedicated to living out the Gospel in fresh ways either in the midst of the world's neediest populations or in other creative expressions. I have long dreamed of a revival of "religious life" (the technical term for monks and nuns and such) in which people would give themselves to a life of Gospel community, simplicity, holiness, and service in the power of the Holy Spirit. Perhaps the first signs of such a revival are showing themselves today.

Consequently, I am concerned for the health of these communities. Such tender souls, with such large hopes and expectations, coming together from such different backgrounds, to accomplish such wonderful things. And yet we are all such difficult people! How can we maintain sufficient harmony, unity, and stability to enable the kinds of investments required to become an authentic force of change in the world? Yes, I believe in the ministry of the Holy Spirit, but just as I employ means of grace to facilitate the work of the Spirit in my personal life, I wonder if there are means of grace that might be employed to facilitate the Spirit's work of healing, building up, and maturing us as local communities of new religious.

I am also aware that a number of historic religious Orders (such as Benedictines, Franciscans, Jesuits and the like) have persevered through many conflicts over many centuries. While the witness of such groups has shined brighter in some seasons more than others, I find traditional religious communities worthy of closer exploration, especially by young evangelical Protestants. There is, I think, much for us to learn therein, even if we do not find ourselves "signing on." What means of grace have helped these communities to maintain their ministries over time?

It was with such interests and concerns in mind that I discovered the Chapter of Faults. The idea of people honestly opening themselves up to one another regularly, breaking down barriers of pride and self-interest in the context of a covenanted community seemed like a perfect means to facilitate a persevering harmony. But the more I investigated the Chapter of Faults, the more faults I found in the practice. And when I tried to resolve the faults while retaining something of the practice (sort-of like "having your cake and eating it, too"!), I found myself enmeshed in complex historical and theological issues.

I have not fully resolved those issues (it may require a serious investigation of the history of the doctrine and practice of penance and of the responses of the different expressions of the sixteenth century Reformations). Nevertheless, it seems worthwhile to offer some "working proposal" for a contemporary practice of a chapter of faults and affirmations to be explored in the context of religious communities today. Perhaps as we explore and communicate we can find out what works best. I will divide my presentation here into three sections. First, I will outline the historical development of the Chapter of Faults, starting with the relevant biblical material. Then I will provide a few descriptions of the practice and its strengths and weaknesses, along with a description of a practice of "affirmation" I have seen. I will conclude with a few principles that might guide this practice today.

HISTORICAL DEVELOPMENT

The practice of the Chapter of Faults has its roots in the biblical injunctions regarding mutual care for one another and for the purity of the Body of Christ. James encourages his readers to "confess your sins to each other and pray for each other so that you may be healed" (James 5:16). Paul speaks of spiritual gifts and spiritual leaders given for the sake of the common good or for the equipping, edifying, and maturing of the body (1 Corinthians 12:7; 14:3-5; Ephesians 4:12-13). He encourages those who are in the Spirit to restore and to discipline those who have fallen into sin (Galatians 6:1; 1 Corinthians 5:1-12; 2 Corinthians 2:5-11). Similarly Jesus outlines a process for navigating faults within the community of believers (Matthew 18:15-35).

A few central principles of community life can be learned from these and other similar passages. First, life together is a salvation-life. We share life together as means of facilitating the maturing of individuals, of the body as a body, and of the work of the kingdom of God more generally. Life together on earth, for Christians, is not merely (or even primarily) about finding cheap rent or common interests. We join lives together for the sake of the Lord's influence over an increasing sphere of reality. Second, our differences contribute both to our problems (envy, factions, self-hatred, and so on) and to our growth (each gift/person expressing a unique aspect of the Spirit of Christ). Third, members of a covenanted community are responsible for each other. The myth of a private life is just that: a myth. We are our kindred's keepers, and God made it that way. Fourth, private sins have public repercussions. What I do in secret does affect the life of the community as a whole, though some sins have more direct on community life than others. Public confession effects the healing of both individual and community. Fifth, forgiveness is important. Jesus's death provided a vehicle for our forgiveness, for our welcome by God. Our experience of God's welcome is connected to our practice of other-welcome. Finally, the means of care (for example, the degrees of warning, punishment, exclusion, readmission and so on) are matters of wisdom related to the restoration of the individual and the purity of the community.

We have reason to believe that public confession was practiced by the Christian church from its earliest centuries. The Didache (perhaps written before the end of the first Christian century), instructs Christians on the Lord's day to "come together, break bread and hold Eucharist, after confessing your transgressions that your offering may be pure; but let none who has a quarrel with his fellow join in your meeting until they be reconciled, that your sacrifice be not defiled" (xiv.1-2). Both Tertullian (c. 160-225) and Cyprian (d. 258) mention the importance of exhomologesis, or the public confession of sin. Accompanying the public confession of sin there developed--even in the first centuries--an expectation of penance, acts performed by the sinners which expressed their regret, encouraged their heartfelt seeking of the help of the Lord, and spurred them on toward transformation. By the fourth century different locations of the church building and various postures of those who committed serious sins were used to identify a progressive movement from punishment/penance toward full reinstitution in the church.

The tension that lies underneath the development of penitential practice in the early church is their understanding of conversion. On the one hand the Church believed that conversion/baptism did something. When we give ourselves to Christ, "there is a new creation." Thus Simon Tugwell speaks of "the venerable tradition in the church according to which the new life which we receive in baptism ought, in principle, to result in a radical and immediate change in our whole attitude and behaviour." (Ways of Imperfection, 37). But what happens when the change is not so radical or immediate? Or how do we foster another's growth in the midst of difficult temptations? How do we feel about the sinful-saved potential of new Christians? Within the context of the local churches, public confession, pastoral care, and penitential policies struggled to shepherd a growing Church into maturity of faith.

In the context of early monastic life, other factors influenced the character of confession and mutual edification. Great respect was given to the martyrs, and this respect was passed along in a similar manner to those who, through withdrawal and/

or severe disciplines, lived a "white martyrdom,"
putting to death all association with the world,
the flesh and the devil. The early Christian ascetics
became regarded as holy people, sought after for
their wisdom and power. A separate "class" of
Christians was developing: (1) the "religious", those
who committed themselves to a life of singlehood,
financial simplicity, and the pursuit of the fullest
possible obedience to the commands of Christ,
and (2) the Christian populus in general, who did
the best they could to follow Christ in the midst of
their families and jobs and secular associations.
Increasingly people came to the early ascetics
for a "word" of salvation. Or they advised one
another. One young monk would manifest his or
her thoughts to an elder as the elder would listen
for the heart of the younger and the voice of the
Spirit. Emphasis was placed on both the high aim
of perfection, and on the gracious, unjudgmental,
wisdom of the elder. Advice and penance was given
one to one with careful discerning of appropriate
measure.

The fact of the matter is that, most probably,
some mixture of private and public confession was
present in both church and monastic settings, but
it is hard to sort out all the evidence for time and
location and situation. What is clear is that in time
communities of monks formed who collected the
sayings and wisdom of the elders who preceded
them. The community context placed less emphasis
on the aggressiveness of personal spiritual
disciplines and more emphasis on the refining
work of community life itself. Ultimately, this

collection of wisdom in the context of communal monasticism becomes the development of the monastic "Rule." In some monasteries, the Rule and the abbot can be seen as the primary vehicles through which maturity and salvation are obtained. Simon Tugwell, speaking of the strictures of the Rule of the Master, writes, "The grounds for the Master's reluctance to allow his monks any freedom of initiative and for his insistence on continual supervision can be found in his profoundly negative view of the human will. He very nearly identifies free will with the will of the flesh, and sees its main function in practice as being to deliver us over to the devil. Salvation is accordingly seen primarily in terms of the denial of our own will, so that we walk 'by someone else's judgment and command'" (Ways of Imperfection, 73).

The Rule of the Master served as one of the models St. Benedict of Nursia used in the writing of his Rule (c. 540). To my knowledge, the primary origin and development of the Chapter of Faults are to be found within the Benedictine Order and the Benedictine Rule. Chapters 23-30 of this Rule address the treatment of disciplinary measures for various transgressions of the monastic community, Rule, and life. The Benedictine Rule, brief and seemingly sharp at times, is actually a humanizing of its predecessors (see Appendix 4 "Disciplinary Measures in the Rule of Benedict" in RB 1980: The Rule of St. Benedict In Latin and English with Notes for an excellent treatment of this). Later on, the Rule states that:"If anyone commits a fault while at any work--while working in the kitchen, in the storeroom, in serving, in the bakery, in the garden, in any craft or anywhere else--either by breaking or losing something or failing in any other way in any other place, he must at once come before the abbot and community and of his own accord admit his fault and make satisfaction. If it is made known through another, he is to be subjected to a more severe correction.When the cause of the sin lies hidden in his conscience, he is to reveal it only to the abbot or to one of the spiritual elders, who know how to heal their own wounds as well as those of others without exposing them and making them public."

The condition implied in this instruction is that there is a time and place for such confessions to be made. Philip Lawrence, OSB, abbot of Christ in the Desert Benedictine Monastery, commenting on this passage specifically mentions a daily chapter as the place for such public confessions of open faults (see http://christdesert.org/Detailed/916.html). Clearly, the Benedictine Rule is careful to make public what needs to be public (even if someone else has to bring it up) and to permit privacy where privacy is needed.

What developed from this regulation in Benedictine history is the practice of a regular "Chapter of Faults." The term "chapter" refers to the gathering of the community for various non-liturgical purposes (instruction, decision-making, discussion of topics, and the like). These meetings were dubbed "chapters" because they would begin with a reading of a chapter of the Rule. The place where they met was likewise named the "chapter-house" or "chapter-room." A portion of the regular meeting [or special meetings] was dedicated to the mutual correction of faults. Lowrie J. Daly, in his Benedictine Monasticism: Its Formation and Development through the 12th Century, describes this portion of a chapter meeting as follows: The monks proceeded to a room near the chapel or church, usually designated as the "chapter room," where a portion of the Rule was read followed by a commentary from the superior, and then faults against the house discipline were confessed or pointed out." (p. 218)

These confessions regarded matters of common and public knowledge--the house rules. At times people owned up to their failures openly. At other times (a situation more severe, because it shows the reluctance of the person at fault to admit what they should have known) someone else had to point out the fault in the presence of the group. Other sorts of failures ("hidden" sins: those which were best not presented in front of the group) were confessed to the abbot or to wise elders. The practice of the chapter of faults spread throughout the monastic world. David Knowles speaks of this practice being employed by the primary abbots of the Cistercians when they met for their periodic business meetings (see his Pachomius to Ignatius, 25). Pierre Mondonnet, in his St. Dominic and His Work mentions that, like other monks, the friars were expected to have "a daily chapter of faults with a code of penance for infractions of the Rule." Likewise, the literature of the devotio moderna of the fourteenth century speaks of "fraternal correction." My suspicion is that we see the

parishes of the middle ages exploring the practice
the practice of private confession, symbolized by
the use of penitential manuals emerging especially
by the Celtic traditions and developed by the
Augustinian canons and other groups. Within
monastic communities, however, the exploration
of private confession was accompanied by a parallel
development and expansion of a form of public
confession centering around the chapter of faults.
Thus the personal confession of minor injuries
affecting the life of the community ("I broke the
mixing bowl yesterday"), expanded to involve any
infraction of the monastic rule of life and involved
the accusations of one member toward another.

Consequently, by the sixteenth century, the
Protestant Reformers felt it necessary to reject
this practice, along with the whole system of
monasticism. Forgiveness, not perfection, was
the effect of the work of Christ. Confession was
also desacralized because of its connection with a
heirarchical understanding of the priesthood. To
the Reformers, our absolution is given by Christ,
not a priest. And yet there was a belief in the
priesthood of all believers. I think that this belief
influenced the development in the Protestant
churches of such practices as Pietist "conventicles,"
Methodist "bands" and other such gatherings (We
might want to explore early Anglican divine Jeremy
Taylor's reflections on the rite of penance here).

The practice of the chapter of faults has waned
among Catholic religious in recent years.
Nonetheless it is still practiced by many today.

THE PRACTICE OF THE CHAPTER
OF FAULTS AND AFFIRMATIONS

Having reviewed a little of the development of the Chapter of Faults, it is now appropriate for us to take a glimpse at what the practice looks like in current monastic practice. I have not done extensive surveys yet, but a few sample descriptions can be found in Marie Thérèse Gass's *Unconventional Women*. Needless to say, these are stories of women who ultimately left religious life, and, consequently, the descriptions reflect their bias. Nonetheless, I think that their descriptions of the meeting itself can give us a flavor of the practice. Later we will turn to an evaluation of the strengths and weaknesses of the Chapter of Faults.

Here is one description of the practice: (**a**) "Nuns entered the chapter room in rank, eyes cast down completely silent, with hands folded under the scapular or tucked into their opposite sleeves. After everyone was seated, the Superior would begin with a prayer. Then individual nuns would rise from their chairs and accuse themselves before everyone of certain faults or infractions of the Rule (Je m' accuse, in French Orders), after which the Superior could ask if anyone else accused that nun of yet other faults. There was no arguing--if someone accused you, you stood accused, and you bowed your head to accept your penance. Penances to be performed could be to recite certain prayers, or a personal act of reparation such as an apology and doing something for the offended person, but often the penances given involved public humiliation in their performance, usually in the refectory during meal time."

And here is another:

(**b**) "The Sisters would file in rank--anybody who was in your convent, and sit facing each other on sides of an aisle (usually 3-4 rows on each side). We had a sermon by the Superior who was sitting at the head of the aisle facing the Sisters, and she would say, "You may begin your accusations," and beginning with the youngest in rank, we'd take turns getting up, going to the middle of the aisle, and accuse ourselves of failing in poverty, (I never heard about chastity) or obedience, or whatever. Then you would say, "Sister, would you please have charity to tell me my faults."

And another:

(**c**) "One at a time by rank, Sisters came forward and knelt in front of the Superior accusing themselves of, e.g. lack of religious decorum by running on the stairs. Then they would ask, "Sister would you have the charity to tell me my faults." Usually two or three Sisters, sometimes more, would stand, and in order of rank, mention a lapse that they'd seen, e.g. "Sister seems to fail in the silence of action by slamming doors." If you'd been next to say the same thing, you sat down. If you'd had something different to say, you said it. This seemed gently done, consistently. We were all under the same rules. once in a great while, no one had anything to say to the kneeling Sister. usually then, the presiding Sister would comment, again, kindly. The Sister next in rank would be standing behind the kneeling one waiting to take her place, so that there were never gaps of waiting. When the Postulants were done, a few words were said to them and they were dismissed. I was impressed when, finally wearing the black habit, I saw the Mistress of Novices, the Superior, and Provincial Superior, and further, the Superior General each had a Sister whose responsibility it was to point out to her her external infractions of the rule. Only once did I hear a Sister mention something that was a matter for confession. Mother Superior stopped her immediately but gently, and told her so."

This last example gives a slightly different picture of the practice:

(**d**) "Our chairs were lined up, eyes lowered as Mother Superior noted deviations from the rule. She didn't name names, but when you recognized yourself, you got up from the chair and kissed the floor. Mother Superior might then give you a penance, and when she released you, you would again kiss the floor. You always kept your eyes lowered during this time."

A few elements are common to all of these accounts. In all but one (**d**), the process involves self-accusation. In all but one (**d**) other sisters have permission to accuse. Penance was mentioned in two of the examples. Clearly the Mother Superior plays an important role in guiding the flow and character of these meetings. What is common to all is that it addresses the faults of the sisters, points at which they have failed to maintain the common values of the Rule. And with this we are led to examine a different example. Here I present my own description of the Church of the Sojourner's practice of common affirmation:

(**e**) It is Sunday evening, the time of the worship service. We are seated in a circle with chairs added in the center to fit everybody. We have taken the first part of our communion (the bread), and have eaten supper together. Perhaps a sermon has been given (periodically the sermon follows the affirmations). The leader for the night will introduce the time of affirmation by saying that this is the time in our week where we say where we've seen God at work in other people's lives. Then the leader will usually offer up one affirmation to prime the pump (for example, "I've seen God at work in you, X, in the way you graciously opened the door for me last night when my arms were full of groceries"). Then another member will offer an affirmation of someone else. A single affirmation usually takes between thirty seconds to a minute to deliver. A wide range of topics are mentioned: someone handled a particular situation well, a conflict was resolved, some grace or gift was expressed and noticed--even the fact that someone is present at the gathering--especially in a time of difficulty-is reason for affirmation. No "cross-talk" is allowed. We simply move from one affirmation to the next. There is no attempt to "cover everybody in the room," but there is a sense of breadth in the offerings. Often the affirmations are divided between a time for children and a time for adults. We realize as we mature in this practice over the years that this time is not merely (or even primarily) about individuals. If we have some private affirmation to offer an individual we are free to give it to her/him in person. We are here in this time to publicly recognize the presence of God at work in the Body of Christ. After somewhere between ten and twenty minutes, depending on the schedule for the night, the person who opened the time closes it, perhaps with a comment that just because we are closing the time does not mean that affirmations can't be given later privately.

With (**e**) we no longer have even the common idea of a mutual confession of faults. Now affirmations are central. And yet there is something similar about this gathering to those we explored earlier. One-by-one people offer brief comments about another (I've not witnessed a self-affirmation yet) and then sit down. The time is short, regular, and important. Like the monastic "chapter of faults," these times are about the community, not just the individuals.

There are strengths and weaknesses of these kinds of sharing. Over time they can become ritual and even trivial (for example, addressing how we open or shut doors). But don't we communicate our relationships with others through the mundane, even trivial, events of the day? Is the triviality a weakness or a strength? There is the vulnerability of being open to the input of your community. This is not easy: in receiving affirmation as well as correction. Yet it is well known that people are devastated by correction much more easily than they are strengthened by affirmation. It takes a number of compliments to balance out one corrective comment. In the traditional chapter of faults, the attention is normally place on infractions of the Rule, not on personal sin. Nevertheless, as one sister put it, "as in everything in life, however, there was overlap, e.g. being angry with someone could be construed as the sin of anger as well as the fault of fault of "failing in charity towards my neighbor." There are sins/faults/affirmations that belong with one's personal spiritual director/confessor and there are others that are very appropriate for the practice of community strengthening. There are appropriate and inappropriate ways of airing our beefs regarding another's annoying habits. Some comments (critical or affirmative) need to be given in an environment where feedback is possible. Other times a grace or concern may be noticed without the need for further comment. Some leaders can use a time like this for gentle formation, modeling the awareness of habits which may not be noticed by others. Other leaders can use a time like this for manipulation and control. And the line between these two is not always clear. Participants must be trained how to offer confession, accusation, and affirmation, or else damage is done to others and to the safety of the community as a whole. I think the combination of heirarchical understandings of leadership, overstereotyped conceptions of holiness, and lack of good training in how to share made the traditional chapter of faults, for many nuns, a damaging rather than a strengthening experience. The context of confession in Scripture (James 5, for example) is clearly a context of mutual strengthening.

A PROPOSAL FOR PRACTICE IN COMMUNITIES TODAY

Which brings us to a proposal for some kind of practice of confession/affirmation today. If I were to summarize the relevant core of this practice as I have explored it so far, it might be something like this: A gathering of mutually committed Christians for the purpose of community strengthening by means of an open sharing of faults or affirmations relevant to our life together.

Let me unpack this.

1. This is a gathering of Christians. By this I mean that love of neighbor, the fruit of the Spirit, and the desire for harmony in difference, are not unfamiliar. We share these values at the core of our very faith. The monastic life assumes the common faith of its members. Those communities who may have some members who "are not believers" will have to deal with this.

2. This is a gathering of mutually committed believers. We are not merely Christians, but Christians related to one another in a certain way. I will be here "with you" and "for you" no matter what you say in this gathering. I am willing to work it out over time. I'm not "out of here" when I have a problem with how things get done. This sense of mutual commitment gives the freedom for difficult things be addressed, for me to open my faults, or to express a deep appreciation at the risk that I may be misunderstood. Religious communities have addressed this with the well-known process of incorporation (postulants, novices, first and final vows). Certain meetings may or may not be

for newcomers who have not made longer term commitments and who have not been trained in this kind of sharing.

3. The faults or affirmations are shared insofar as they are relevant to life together. Monastic communities see this in terms of using the Chapter of Faults as a place where the infractions of the common Rule are addressed. The community has a common set of values and life practices in the Rule that are assumed and valued by all. Some communities do not need as rigid a regulation as that prescribed by some Rules or Constitutions. Nonetheless, as members of a committed community, we all know, to one degree or another, what we expect of each other and our community strengthening confessions and affirmations can be evaluated in this light.

There are times and settings where the focus is on the spiritual formation of members. And this element is present in the monastic practice. There is the confessing and praying for another for the sake of the other's healing. There is the place for private confession, twelve-step support groups, small ministry prayer teams, confessors, mentors, and other forms of supportive relationship. And it is true, that the growth of individuals contributes to the health of the body in general. Nevertheless, there is also a time for sharing what is relevant for life together, and I have a suspicion that care needs to be given in order to guard and nurture this kind of a gathering/sharing for the strengthening of the community.

4. The most basic characteristic of this gathering is that it is a time of open sharing of faults and affirmations. We gather together. We open in prayer, in song, in sacrament, or in hearing. And then we listen. We open ourselves to one another, permitting ourselves to be moved by another. This is listening, allowing the Other (human person) to shape me/us, allowing the Other to be a vehicle of the divine Other (Spirit of God) in my/our life. It is precisely this vulnerability--in the context of mutual commitment--that offers such potential for growth and harmony. I suspect that a variety of different forms can be used to embody such a practice. One must find the form in the context of one's appropriate setting in life. That is a matter of experimentation and revision.

5. But (finally) why do we admit a personal fault, or mention a failing of another [which, by the way, I would only imagine as a rare thing], or share an affirmation of another? I think, in the kind of gathering I am imagining, that this sharing is done so that we all might see one another a bit more for who we are (and this is true of both confessions and affirmations), that we all might affirm who we are as a community, and that we might grow in love. We expose ourselves to this kind of vulnerability in order to strengthen the community. We strengthen one another in order to strengthen the other. We strengthen one another also in order to strengthen one another.

In conclusion, I am thrilled by, and concerned for, the revival of new religious life springing up today.

I am glad to see many who are giving themselves to a nurturing of community, simplicity, service, and holiness in the power of the Spirit. One practice that I suspect might contribute to the health and vitality of these communities is some form of a practice of mutual confession and affirmation. I'm not really certain what that practice might look like in different settings. Still, I offer these reflections in hopes that others will experiment and share wisdom in the years ahead.

6.3 WHAT IS SPIRITUAL DIRECTION?

David Nixon

Defined most simply, Christian spiritual direction is a form of pastoral guidance that fosters in the believer an intimate communion with God the Father. Growth in this communion is shaped through contemplation of Jesus, is guided by the Spirit, and is the close observation of one's life coupled with prayer. The *modus operandi* for developing this intimate communion is through regular meetings of conversation and prayer where one believer (the spiritual director) helps another believer (the directee) to notice the work of God in his/her life and respond to it as promptly, vigorously, joyfully and consistently as possible. The desire of the director is for the directee to experience "christification" — transformation into the image of Christ — and grow in all dimensions of love: in the capacity to receive and enjoy the love of the Father and to offer that love to others. Succinctly put, spiritual direction is a robust form of pastoral care that helps the believer abide in Christ, to remain attached to the True Vine and live fruitfully.[18]

In the Christian tradition we confess that we have seen and experienced God most fully in the person of Jesus. We hear him say, "If you have seen me you have seen the Father." We hear Paul say, "He is the exact image of the invisible God." We hear John say, "In him we found life!" Spiritual direction, then, is about entering the Way of Jesus. It's about being rooted in a "gospel life". This is why the

---

18   John 15:4

contemplation of Christ is central to the practice of spiritual direction.

We also confess that the Holy Spirit (ongoing presence of Jesus) is present in the believer to guide, convict, soften, deepen understanding, instruct and grow virtue in the believer.[19] Whatever concerns we may have about the potential risks of wading into something that can, admittedly, feel very subjective and loose, we affirm that the importance of growing in knowledge and experience regarding the Spirit's role as Advocate. Consequently, learning to notice how the Spirit communicates to and guides us (in and apart from Scripture) is important to the work of spiritual direction.

We also acknowledge that the obvious starting point for understanding the work of God and the movement of the Holy Spirit is the life we have: not the one we used to have or the one we wish we had, but the life we actually have. Furthermore, we are drawn in spiritual direction to notice our reactions to this life and how God might be using it to draw us deeper into his love, more in conformity to Jesus. In spiritual direction we pray through the life we have and our responses to it, looking for will and pleasure of God. Prayer in its more simple and classical formulation — I close my eyes, fold my hands and offer up words directly to God — and more broad and biblical formulations — the sum total of all my verbal and nonverbal responses to God in the life we're given — is the fulcrum by which God harvests our lives.

---

19   1 Corinthians 3.17-18; Luke 12.12; John 15.26; Romans 5.5; 1 Corinthians 6.19; 1 Corinthians 1.10-16 2

The role of the director is not to teach (in the explicit sense of the word) but to provide a safe, focused, guided and contemplative environment in which the directee can explore the relationship with God in all it's complexity. This doesn't mean the director never teaches. Direct teaching is sometimes appropriate and needed, but it is typically rare. However, indirect teaching occurs constantly in that the director models prayer, humility before God, hope, patience, acceptance, lovingkindness, faithfulness, and any number of other virtues. And by her non-anxious, self-differentiated presence, the director provides a powerful though subtle witness to what it means to be rooted in one's identity as a child of God.

The Benedictine monk and author Thomas Merton said that spiritual direction is impossible without a full "manifestation of conscience" on the part of the directee.[20] What he meant was that unless the directee is willing to share the deepest part of self, to confess and lay bare the thoughts of the mind, the movements of the heart, the deepest longings and most intimate questions he holds, spiritual direction will go nowhere. This is principally what we have in mind when we talk about the director providing a safe environment: one in which complete confidentiality is observed. But we also mean it is safe in that the director is never surprised, startled, or put off by the directee. There is a surplus of love and encouragement for the directee, an abundance in which trust can grow.

---

20 Spiritual Direction and Meditation, Thomas Merton

The spiritual director also provides and focused and guided experience. Spiritual direction is not about coaching or mentoring or discipling (as they're normally understood). It's about paying attention to one's experience of God in life and prayer. A good director keeps the focus tight and gently guides the directee back to the principal purpose.

In this tight focus prayer is critical. Prayer is the principal medium through which we understand our lives, by which we initiate, maintain and end all our work on earth. We're encouraged to persevere in prayer and pray at all times. We're pushed to cast all our anxieties and cares on the Lord. It's how we grow into the intimate communion of love that is the terminal point of spiritual direction. This is why directors begin, end and punctuate their sessions with prayer.

In conclusion it seems good to say that spiritual direction, a contemplative form of pastoral care, is in alignment with the Vineyard's DNA and ethos. We refer to ourselves as "a kingdom movement" rather than a mission movement, prophetic movement, or a signs and wonders movement. Our desire is for God's kingdom and God's will to "come on earth as in heaven." We speak of the need for both Presence and Power. These are simply two sides of the same coin. The contemplative and the charismatic are cut from the same cloth: the desire to "see what the Father is doing" and join in that work. To this end spiritual direction is a form of pastoral care that amplifies the Vineyard's self-understanding.

6.4 WHAT IS A RULE OF LIFE?

Evan B. Howard[21]

Perhaps we should really ask a different question: "What is life?" When we ask that question we can talk about flourishing, about energy, about sustaining, or even just about heart-beats and brain-waves. But whenever we talk about life, we must talk about some kind of order that characterizes that life. Brain waves are structured in a particular way, or else there is a problem. Photosynthesis in plants, and breathing, digestion, and such in animals are ordered to enable the sustaining of life. When I tell someone that I have been flourishing lately--or that I have been "living it up"--I usually have in mind certain moods, habits, activities, or events that characterize "life." Life has order. The very orders of life are what *make them* life. So should we be asking about a rule of life, or about life itself and the order or rules that give life?

What is a Rule of Life, particularly with regard to Christians? Author and spiritual guide Marjorie Thompson, defines a rule of life as "a pattern of spiritual disciplines that provides structure and direction for growth in holiness."[22] Stephen Macchia,

---

21 I have written this essay as an accompaniment to my videos "Rules of Life: A Brief Introduction" (https://www.youtube.com/watch?v=ExYD9vW4eGE) and "EvansRule2" (https://www.youtube.com/watch?v=7pl2y1h3b-g). The is essay is not, however, the script to the videos, but is rather a written compliment to the video presentation. For more old monastic wisdom for new monastic people see under "Resources" at spiritualityshoppe.org.

22 Marjorie Thompson, Soul Feast: An Invitation to the Christian Spiritual Life (Westminster/John Knox, 1995/2005), 146.

also an author and leadership trainer, defines a
rule of life as "a holistic description of the Spirit-
empowered rhythms and relationships that create,
redeem, sustain and transform the life God invites
you to humbly fulfill for God's glory."[23] I like to think
of a Rule of Life as *a concrete expression of the life-intentions
of a Christian community or individual made in order to help
maintain or mature relationship with God and the Gospel.*
Rules of Life have special relevance for people who
make special commitments of faith. To understand
this better, I think it helps to see the history and
structure of Rules of Life.

SCRIPTURE

In the Bible, we see an early reference to something
like a Rule of Life in the regulations for the
Nazarites outlined in Numbers 6. The Nazarites
were individuals who offered themselves in
complete consecration to God. As part of their life of
consecration, Nazarites abstained from wine, kept
their hair long and stayed clear of dead bodies. We
also catch a glimpse of an Old Testament clan with
similar commitments when we read of the devout
nomads, the Rechabites in Jeremiah 35. I suspect
that there was also some life-ordering component
involved in the development of the "schools of the
prophets" (see 1 Samuel 19:18-21; 2 Kings 2:5-7;
Isaiah 8:16).

Nearer the time of Jesus, one of the communities
of Jews often called "Essenes" outlined their way
of life in what has been named the Qumran Rule

---

23 Stephen Macchia, *Crafting A Rule of Life: An Invitation to the
Well-Ordered Way* (Downers Grove, IL: InterVarsity Press,
2012), 14.

Scroll. This Rule Scroll gives a description of the ideals of the community, a ceremony of initiation, general wisdom regarding values central to the community, and particular regulations regarding relationships, ministries, property and their life together. Another similar group existing around the same time were the more contemplative "Therapeutae," mentioned in the writings of Philo and others, and we can glean something of their Rule of Life by reading these ancient writings.

When Jesus sent out his followers to minister in the villages surrounding him, he gave them an outline of their way of life (see Matthew 10; Mark 6:6-13; Luke 9-10). He identified their mission (heal, deliver, proclaim) and gave them instructions regarding possessions, relationships and ministry activities. In the context of Jesus's own culture, this would have been understood as a Rule of Life, a way of structuring the life-intentions of a given group of people who are (in this case, temporarily) making special commitments to serve God.

Later in the book of Acts we read about the elders who give themselves "to prayer and the ministry of the word" (Acts 6:4). Similarly, in Acts 13 we heard of the Holy Spirit asking the church at Antioch to "set apart" Paul, Barnabas, and later others for apostolic ministry. And when we read the epistles, we find not a formal Rule, but at least hints of principles regarding work, marriage and such which the apostolic communities used to guide their traveling ministries.

Finally, I think it is also fair to see, in the comments regarding widows who "continues night and day to pray" found in 1 Timothy 5, at least a seed of the order of widows which developed much more formally in succeeding centuries.[24]

CHURCH HISTORY

We have evidence of groups of widows and virgins from the early centuries of the Christian Church. What we call "monasticism" or "religious life" probably developed from these beginnings. Antony of Egypt, one of the pioneers of Christian monasticm, developed his own way of life by the careful observation of his elders.

He observed the graciousness of one, the eagerness for prayers in another; he took careful note of one's freedom from anger, and the human concern of another. And he paid attention to one while he lived a watchful life, or one who pursued studies, as also he admired one for patience, and another for fastings and sleeping on the ground. . . . And having been filled in this manner, he returned to his own place of discipline, from that time gathering the attributes of each in himself, and striving to manifest in himself what was best from all.[25]

---

24 A more complete treatment of religious life in Scripture would need to address Jesus's encouragements to voluntary simplicity, various discussions of celibacy, other particular disciplines such as fasting and prayer, along with some broader concerns. I am here only offering a few notes related to a few passages.

25 Athanasius, Life of Antony #4. This work is found in many editions. I am citing from Robert C. Gregg, translator, Athanasius: the Life of Antony and the Letter to Marcellinus (New York: Paulist Press, 1980), 32-33.

Use of the term "Rule" to describe a concrete expression of Christian life-intentions developed particularly in the fourth century. The biography of Pachomius, a pioneer in Christian community life, speaks of his care for the community stating "Our father Pachomius was working at the salvation of the brother's souls as at a vineyard cared for by a good and industrious gardener. . . . For he gave them laws and traditions; some were committed to writing, some others were learned by heart, after the manner of the holy Gospels of Christ."[26] Evagrius, a monk and spiritual theologian, encourages his monastic readers that, Evagrius, *Praktikos* #40, "One is not always in a position to follow his usual rule of life but one must always be on the alert to seize the opportunities to fulfill all the duties possible to the best of his powers."[27] Followers of Basil the Great collected a list of Frequently Asked Questions regarding the life of the communities he led. This list was published and ultimately became known as the *Ascetikon* or the Rule of Basil.[28] Melania the younger wrote a Rule of

---

26   "The Bohairic Life," The Life of Saint Pachomius and His Disciples translated by Armand Veilleux, Volume 1 (Kalamazoo, Michigan, 1980), p. 145.

27   Evagrius, Praktikos (The Practical Life), #40. This work is found in various collections of Evagrius' writings. I am citing from John Eudes Bamberger, translator, The Praktikos, Chapters on Prayer (Kalamazoo, Michigan: Cistercian Publications, 1981), p. 27. See also the various references to "rule" in Benedicta Ward, editor, The Lives of the Desert Fathers: The Historia Monachorum in Aegypto (Kalamazoo, Michigan, 1980), pp. 65, 69, 88. 96.

28   See Anna M. Silvas, The Ascetikon of St. Basil the Great (Oxford: Oxford University Press, 2005), 2.

Life for her community in Jerusalem.[29] I could go on and on from here.

The writing of Rules as a means of securing life for communities and individuals developed wherever Christians wanted to make special commitments to God. Some of the most influential Rules in Christiandom have been the Augustinian Rule, the Rule of Benedict, and the Franciscan Rule. Giorgio Agamben reflects on the phrase "rule and life" used by Francis of Assisi stating that Francis, in calling the rule, "not only rule but life, intended to clarify the sense of the rule, which is a right form of life and a life-giving rule that leads to the life of Christ. Such a rule does not consist in a written text, but in the act and in the operation of life and does not dissolve into an obligation and profession of vows."[30]

The Protestant Reformation brought radical changes to the institutions of monasticism. On the one hand, some Protestant reformers closed many monasteries. On the other hand Anabaptists, for example, developed "Ordnungen" to give shape to their way of life. Other Protestant communities (such as the Moravian Brethren, Puritans, Methodists) developed "covenants," "resolutions," and "instituted means of grace" in order to respond

---

29 Laura Swan, The Forgotten Desert Mothers: Sayings, Lives, and Stories of Early Christian Women (Mahwah, New Jersey: Paulist Press, 2001), 145.

30 Giorgio Agamben, The Highest Poverty: Monastic Rules and Form-of-Life, translated by Adam Kotsko (Stanford, CA: Stanford University Press, 2013), 107. Here Agamben is actually summarizing and reflecting on an early commentary of Francis's writings by Olivi, who he quotes and summarizes in my citation above.

to a similar impulse.[31] To make a long story short, there are groups and individuals who follow formal Rules of Life in virtually all branches Christianity today.

STRUCTURE: CONTENT AND FORM

Now that we see how Rules of Life have been used to order--and thus to facilitate--Christian life, we are ready to examine just what a Rule of life *is*: how it is structured and what the form and contents are like. I have examined the contents and form of a number of Rules and such elsewhere.[32] Though the length, style, and particulars of Rules of Life can vary a great deal, most Rules say something about a few key matters.

Rules often begin with some statement of vision. What are we about? (or "What am I about," if this is a personal rule) Where are we going? The Rule of Benedict begins with a call to courageous commitment, urging the readers to put into action the teachings of the Gospel. "Therefore we intend to establish a school for the Lord's service. . . . Do not be daunted immediately by fear and run away from the road that leads to salvation. . . . But as we progress in this way of life and in faith, we shall run on the path of God's commandments,

---

31 For this history, see, for example, Ivan J. Kauffman, Follow Me: A History of Christian Intentionality (Eugene, Oregon: Wipf and Stock, 2009); and Greg Peters, Reforming the Monastery: Protestant Theologies of the Religious Life (Cascade Books, 2013).

32 See my "A Collection of Tables of Contents from Rules, Covenants, Constitutions and Such" at http://spiritualityshoppe.org/wp-content/uploads/2013/01/rules1.pdf. accessed 4/18/14. Pay careful attention to the summary at the end.

our hearts overflowing with the inexpressible delight of love."[33] The opening lines of the 1221 Rule of the Franciscans declare that, "The Rule and life of the friars is to live in obedience, in chastity, and without property, following the teaching and the footsteps of our Lord Jesus Christ."[34] The 1727 "Brotherly Union and Agreement" of the Moravian Brethren, after proclaiming that their existence owes to God's grace, states that "Herrnhut, and its original old inhabitants must remain in a constant bond of love with all children of God belonging to the different religious persuasions--they must judge none, . . . but rather seek to maintain among themselves the pure evangelical doctrine, simplicity, and grace."[35] A school of Christian obedience, a family of radical Jesus-followers, an Gospel ecumenical welcome center: In each Rule, the basic vision of the community or individual is expressed. We might want to communicate a more general vision: what we sense God's plan is all about. Or we might want to express a more particular vision: a sense of where God is calling *us* right here and now. Some Rules don't start with

---

33 Rule of Benedict, Prologue 45-49. There are many editions of Benedict's Rule. I am citing from Timothy Fry, editor, RB 1980: The Rule of St. Benedict In Latin and English with Notes (Collegeville, MN: The Liturgical Press, 1981), p. 165.

34 Francis of Assisi, "Rule of 1221" (also known as the Regula non Bullata) Chapter 1. I am citing from Marion A. Habig, editor, St. Francis of Assisi: Wrtings and Early Biographies: English Omnibus of the Sources for the Life of St. Francis (Chicago, Illinois: Franciscan Herald Press, 1983), p. 31.

35 Nicolas Ludwig, Count von Zinzendorf, "Brotherly Union and Agreement at Herrnhut" #2 in Peter C. Erb, editor, Pietists: Selected Writings (New York: Paulist Press, 1983), p. 325.

a vision statement at all. The vision just grows over time in the midst of the practice of life.

Another matter that is often discussed in Rules of Life is rhythm. "What we do with our life" and "what we do with our time" are intimately connected. Consequently Rules frequently give voice to an individual or communities intentions with regard to use of time. Times of prayer, work, study, community, ministry are often specified, in various degrees of detail. The Augustinian *Ordo Monasterii*, for example, after providing a list of the Psalms and readings to be used at the various times of prayer throughout the day states that the monks "are to work from early morning to the sixth hour and then let them have time for reading from the sixth hour to the ninth."[36]

Most Rules treat a number of what I call "ordinary matters." They discuss how counsel is to be made, terms of leadership, eating and fasting, sleeping arrangements, care of the sick, distribution of possessions, clothing, use of transportation and all kinds of details. But this is no minor matter because, as we all know, life is in the details, is it not? It is surprising how petty the matters are that Satan can use can divide us as communities or distract us as individuals. The fifth-century Rule of the Four Fathers, for example, states regarding the monks' use of common property, that "whatever is used in the monastery, whether in the form of

---

36 "The Ordo Monasterii" #2-3 in Saint Augustine, The Monastic Rules, edited by Boniface Ramsey and translated by Sister Agatha Mary and Gerald Bonner (Hyde Park, New York: New City Press, 2004), p. 106.

vessels or tools or all other things, is consecrated. If anyone has used something negligently, he should realize that . . . he deserves such a punishment"[37]

Finally, there are "inner matters" that must be addressed. Arrangements for spiritual guidance, acknowledgment of virtues that are vital to the individual or the community, identification of situations and conditions within which the wiles of the enemy might try to gain ground: all of these and more are touched on in our Rules of Life. Salome Sticken's "A Way of Life for Sisters" summarizes the inner spirit of their common life by remind her sisters that "to sense and to taste the sweetness of the Lord God is highly delightful, but the foundation of all sanctity lies rather in complete self-denial, mortification of the evil affections in our corrupt natures, and the conversion of our will to the Lord n an effort to conform it totally to his will."[38] The A Rule of Life is a good place to recognize together the work of God (and the enemy) within us and to plan appropriate responses.

MOVING FROM THE GENERAL TO THE SPECIFICS OF ONE'S LIFE

A Rule of Life can be a source of life. It can also become a stifling strait-jacket. There is a wisdom to developing and living a Rule of Life. Part of the

---

37 The Rule of the Four Fathers, chapter 12, in Carmela Vircillo Franklin, Ivan Havener, and J. Alcuin Francis, translators, Early Monastic Rules: The Rules of the Fathers and the Regula Orientalis (Collegeville, Minnesota: The Liturgical Press, 1982), p. 27.

38 Salome Sticken, "A Way of Life for Sisters" in John van Engen, translator, Devotio Moderna: Basic Writings (New York: Paulist Press, 1988), p. 184.

wisdom is learning how to shape the broad and general guidelines into the narrow and concrete realities of your life. I offer a few suggestions.

First, at the start of your exploration of a Rule, keep track of your time, your life. When you have learned what the honest realities of your life schedule, emotional energies, relationships and such demand, you will be best equipped to shape a Rule of Life that reflects, not merely a pious ideal, but the concrete shape of life as you live it (as a community or as an individual). For example, I moved to Colorado with the hope of establishing something of a rhythm of prayer, work, study, and people-ministry. I tried making particular days set aside for study or work. The problem was, however, that the weather and other factors did not always cooperate. After a season of documenting my activities I learned to order my rhythm, not by a precise schedule, but rather by a tracking of the percentage of my time used for various activities. I was able to maintain the general values of my rhythm, but to live them out within my own changing world of ranching, teaching, writing, and so on.

Second, start small. I think it is better to develop slowly, constantly longing for more, than to aim too high and fail, giving up all hope for the future. This is why there is the progression from postulant, to novice, to full member. You can stick your toe into the water before you dive in.

Third, develop your more specified Rule in dialogue with key friends and mentors. If it is a personal Rule, believe me, others who love you will be able to spare you from much harm if you let them speak into your life. If it is a common Rule of Life, take note: often those who are permitted to shape the common life, have the strongest buy-in to that life.

Finally, learn to trust God through experimenting and revising your Rule. Become like a child, and play! What diet is appropriate for you? This depends on your work, your health, your own history of relationship with food and more. So often we just simply follow the diet trends of those around us without ever seriously considering how we relate to food. So why not start exploring by experimenting? Change your diet this way or that way. Listen to the voice of the Spirit (and wise friends) as you "play with your food". Our eating is basic to our living (duh?). So learn how to give yourself fully to God in this area of life--and indeed with all areas of life--by prayerful play. And as you do, remember that God loves you and has a wonderful plan for your life.

What is a Rule of Life? It is life itself, a concrete expression of a new form of life, inspired by the Spirit of Christ, empowered by the Grace of Christ, in obedience to the Word of Christ. Through our little Rules of life, we learn to follow the Rules of the Scripture and Spirit, which leads us--as best we can--to embody the supreme Rule of Christ and the Gospel.

APPENDICES

81201822R00066

Made in the USA
Lexington, KY
16 February 2018